Awards and Recognition for *I Can See for Miles*

Hollie Stuart's moving memoir *I Can See for Miles* has garnered numerous national and international accolades for its compelling and evocative storytelling.

Winner of the 2023 Independent Authors Network Book of the Year Awards in the Outstanding General Nonfiction category

Finalist in two more categories of nonfiction in the 2023 Independent Authors Network Book of the Year Awards

Finalist for Best Nonfiction in the 2023 Kindle Book Awards

Finalist for Best Nonfiction in the 2023 International Book Awards

Finalist for Best Nonfiction in the 2023 Indie Excellence Awards

Finalist in three categories of nonfiction for the 2023 Next Generation Indie Book Awards

Winner in two categories of Nonfiction for the 2023 BookFest® Awards

Finalist for Best Nonfiction in the 2023 Oklahoma Book Awards

#1 Bestseller in Nonfiction for state of Oklahoma in April 2023

#1 Amazon Bestseller for November 2023

I CAN SEE FOR MILES

Overcoming the Past and Running to My Future

HOLLIE STUART

ISBN: 978-1-7372742-1-6 (Paperback)
ISBN: 978-1-7372742-0-9 (Hardcover)

Library of Congress Control Number: 2022919367

Book cover design by Victoria Wolf.
Typesetting and interior design by Crystal MM Burton.

Printed by Marathon Publishing Co., in the United States of America.

First printing edition 2022.

Marathon Publishing Co.
3000 W. Memorial Rd, Suite 123, No. 115
Oklahoma City, OK 73120

For anyone who has suffered in silence and shame . . .
May you find your way back to your light.

AUTHOR'S NOTE

Memoirs are, of course, based on memories. Where I could, I revisited photographs, videos, and journal entries to provide the reader with the most accurate account of events based on my experiences. For the rest, I attempted to adhere to the truth of my memories as best as I could. Most dialogue, of course, has been reconstructed with only the most vital parts of conversations. In some cases, I condensed chronology and dialogue for the sake of narrative pacing. In addition, I changed some names and did not disclose others to protect people's privacy.

TABLE OF CONTENTS

FOREWORD

By Jill Keuth

In January 2017, I conducted a thirty-day series of Facebook Lives. At that time, I had been a life coach for two years and, on a whim, decided to livestream every evening to share insights and wisdom I had learned and applied to my life and shared with my clients. I invited women like me who were perhaps feeling disconnected, whose happiness, peace, and fulfillment eluded them no matter how hard they tried or how hard they worked. I encouraged them to be curious and suggested small ways they could shift their perceptions of themselves and their lives. I wanted to help women realize they are more than what they do or have done, what they have or don't have, what people think of them, and what happened to them. If doing a video every evening could pique women's curiosity that maybe they had more inside of them to be actualized, perhaps together, we could make the world a better place.

Hollie became one of "the regulars," tuning in with me live every evening. After the series ended, I wasn't surprised when Hollie reached out to me to explore coaching. Our journey together to help reconnect her to her True Self and become who she is meant to be began that February and continued for a few years.

Hollie and I were born ten days apart. We came of age in the '80s, the decade that was pop culture heaven. While creating our own adventures or playing sports outside occupied our early years, the cool toys, video games, movies, TV shows, and MTV made a huge mark on our identity as Gen Xers.

My and Hollie's paths first crossed during high school from 1989–1993 at a small Catholic school in Oklahoma City. Hollie and I were not friends in high school, not because we wouldn't have gotten along or enjoyed each other's company. It was more of a proximity issue. I don't remember having any classes together. Hollie was in all advanced courses, and I wasn't. Hollie was a member of the state champion cross country team, and I wasn't. I looked up to the phenomenal young women and men who ran cross country. I admired how hard-working, determined, and focused they were. I assumed Hollie and her teammates felt self-assured, happy, and on top of the world. Running miles together day after day, year after year, they had a close bond and camaraderie that I longed for myself. In her story, Hollie sees it differently. From her perspective, I was in the "cool crowd." At forty-seven, this was news to me, as I have never felt, seen, or described myself as "cool."

Perception is a tricky thing. Left unchecked, we can easily take our perceptions—our thoughts and opinions of ourselves and others—at face value. This unconscious programming gets passed down to us or ingrained in us by the families, cultures, religions, and societies we are raised in and around. This is most problematic when we form our perceptions of ourselves. In other words, based on that programming, we make up stories about who we are or what other people think of us, and *we believe those stories*.

When I first started working with Hollie, she was deeply disconnected from her core, her true Essence. She based her perceptions of herself on what she had done or not done in her life and, more painfully, on what happened to her—especially the correlation she made between external circumstances and traumatic events against her own worth and value. Having navigated a similar, yet different, identity crisis years before, I knew the power of rediscovering one's True Self and built a coaching modality around it.

The truth is every single one of us is navigating this life journey that is filled with good times, hard times, and painful, traumatic moments. Of course, we see differing degrees of trauma. However, there is no way to compare trauma, suffering, and pain. It is incredibly personal. What is so distressing is that many of us are conditioned to think what happens to us is our fault. We take on shame and keep our pain silent and in the dark, as Hollie had done for most of her life.

In Hollie's story, she reminds us that life brings us trials and tribulations, seemingly at every turn. One will experience the highest of highs and the lowest of lows in her life. This pendulum of big wins and seemingly significant losses is a theme throughout Hollie's struggle with the ups and downs. I experienced a visceral desire for a linear experience, for certainty, and a straightforward redemption story. *Go through the hard time, learn the lesson, climb the mountain, rejoice, and you've done it! All happiness and smooth sailing from here.* I caught myself and remembered, *That is not how life works.*

Hollie is a woman who has fought for herself time and again throughout her life. Finding her way back to herself was no different. Hollie shows us in her book that joy, happiness, and a meaningful life are not something we seek outside of us; rather, they must be cultivated within us. Deep within Hollie, there has always been an adventurous spirit who encouraged her to keep going, not only in the Osage Hills around Pawhuska, Oklahoma, but on the highest peaks of our world. And while many of us may never climb Mount

Kilimanjaro or run a marathon, Hollie reminds us we are worth climbing our own mountains, running our own races, and awakening to our own life journeys. No one ever said life was going to be easy. Hollie powerfully demonstrates that sometimes, like climbing a mountain or running a race, we must take one step forward and two steps back with our own healing to keep moving forward. She shows us that life is always happening for us, and we have helpers, guides, and encouragers along the way. We have only to believe we are worthy of the adventure and remember we don't have to go it alone.

Hollie and I live in different states now, and our primary connection is back to where we began in 2017—through Facebook. Connecting on social media with Hollie not only makes the platform more tolerable, but it also brings joy to my life. I am so grateful Hollie believed in herself and was willing to work so hard to release many layers of programming and conditioning. Hollie created miracles in her life, powerfully shifted her perceptions of herself, and ultimately found her way back to her Essence. Following Hollie is sure to lift anyone's spirits. A beacon of positivity and humor, Hollie not only makes you smile, but she'll have you craving pizza, creating a bucket list of places around the world you hope to visit someday, and feeling inspired by—and living vicariously through—her walks, runs, and bike rides. Most of all, Hollie's tenacity and resilience to get back up and keep going encourages me to do the same in my own life.

— **Jill Keuth**, *Life Coach and Founder of Be Courageously You*

PROLOGUE

Stone Town, Zanzibar, Tanzania
July 2017

I HAVE BEEN KIDNAPPED. WHEN I awoke this morning, I didn't imagine I would be cruising across the Indian Ocean in a rickety skiff with two strange men to a place called Prison Island. *Prison Island? What was I thinking?* When I signed up for this excursion, I envisaged sailing with a group of Western tourists to the island in an opulent, enclosed vessel, like the one I took from mainland Italy to Venice a year before. This was no modern cruiser; on the contrary, it was a simple wooden craft tacked together with crude scraps of lumber and nails. My local tour guide Newman, a young, jovial Tanzanian, led me to the beach, where workers hammered slats of wood together for similar vessels. I stared at the boat bobbing in the glistening water. *I'm going to get in* that *thing?*

"I don't see a dock," I told Newman. "How are we climbing onboard?"

He smiled and nodded toward the boat. "Just roll up your pants and wade through the water."

That wasn't what I had in mind, but all right. I had roughed it on Mount Kilimanjaro and out in the Serengeti over the past couple of weeks, where full gales caked my slick skin with dirt and grime. *I guess I can do this.*

I rolled up my capris, slung my bag over my shoulder, and plowed through the water. Aside from Newman and the captain, I was the only passenger. The captain, his ebony skin weatherworn from the sun and sea, affixed the motor to the back of the boat and tugged the cord. As it roared to life, he jumped onboard.

Newman pointed to a speck on the horizon. "See the island?" he asked. "It will take us about forty-five minutes to get there."

As I clenched the side of the ramshackle boat, I pondered all my crazy, often spontaneous, exploits. I thought back to the time in Morocco I explored an abandoned kasbah in the Sahara Desert eight years earlier, the full moon casting its shadow on the labyrinthine walls of the ancient fortress. That was fantastic! I got to pretend I was a female Indiana Jones! I thought about the time I went skydiving from ten thousand feet a few months before, which, oddly enough, was not daunting to me. Even scaling Mount Kilimanjaro, the tallest freestanding mountain in the world, a week before did not intimidate me.

Of course, the two weeks I had already spent exploring the remote parts of Tanzania did not frighten me, either. As part of an organized tour, I felt safe within the sanctuary of my group. This venture to Prison Island was different, however. I was no longer enveloped in the safety of my new friends. I was truly traveling alone. When I planned this voyage, I knew it was risky to separate from my tour group on mainland Tanzania to travel to Zanzibar. Still, I had read so many wonderful reviews about the island, I wanted to experience it while I was nearby. Besides, I had ventured to other places by myself, such as England or Iceland, but they were relatively safe for a woman to travel solo, and I could blend in well. Not so in

Tanzania. I was a tall white woman, and my appearance garnered the attention of the domineering street vendors, who swarmed me, hoping I would purchase their sundry goods. I held up my palm and exclaimed, "*Hapana asante,*" which means, "No thank you," in Swahili. No, this was not Western Europe, where I could camouflage myself. In Europe, I fit in so well the townspeople often mistook me for a local.

It didn't help that my trip from mainland Tanzania to the island of Zanzibar started with complications. When I took a taxi from my hotel in Moshi to the airport in Arusha, I spent the last of my cash on the one-hour ride. Once I reached Kilimanjaro International Airport, it took another hour to work through security with all my luggage. I had no choice but to carry all the gear I used to climb Mount Kilimanjaro. When I appeared at the check-in counter, I heaved my bags on the scale, where the attendant weighed my luggage. It exceeded the allowed weight limit of 25 kilograms (56 pounds).

"That will be 125,000 shillings or $54," he said in his Tanzanian accent.

I panted. "I don't have any cash. Do you take cards?"

"No, we just take cash, ma'am."

"Do you have an ATM?" I asked.

"We have one outside. You can try it, but you must go back through security."

I glanced at the long line I had just treaded. *Crap!*

"It took me an hour to make it through before. If I have to go through again, I'll miss my flight. Can someone please escort me out there and back through?"

He called someone on his radio in Swahili. "Okay, this gentleman will go out there with you."

We returned to the passenger drop-off, where he escorted me

to an ATM. I followed the instructions on the screen, only to find the machine did not work.

"It doesn't always behave," he said. "I will take you to another one."

I tried the second one. Just as I thought it was about to dispense money, a message appeared saying it was out of funds.

I ran my fingers through my dirty blonde hair. "It's out of money. What else can I do?"

"You can take a cab to an ATM away from the airport."

"I don't have money for a cab. And if I do that, I will miss my flight." I did not want to spend the night alone in a tiny foreign airport.

He accompanied me back to the ticket counter, where I spoke again with the agent.

"I tried both ATMs, and they don't work. Is there *any* way you can let me on the flight? I'll get cash and pay you when I get to Zanzibar."

"Okay," he said. "I will let you on with your bags and call the airport."

"Thank you so much! I really appreciate this!" I sighed with relief as the agent checked my bags and let me board the plane.

Once the jet lifted off, the sun crept below the horizon, darkness gathering at the tip of the plane's wings. The flight attendant announced our arrival in Swahili only minutes later while twilight faded into black. As often as I had traveled, I had never entered a foreign country at nighttime, much less by myself. Usually, the sight of the unexplored terrain or the distant city below enlivened me. Instead, I peered out at nothing but shadows, the obscurity putting me on edge.

When I stepped off the plane, a skycap approached me. "Do

you need assistance?"

"I just need to claim my bags."

I showed him my passport, and he said, "Oh yes, you need to pay the baggage fee."

They don't kid around here.

He guided me to the closest ATM. As before, I tried to access money, but it too was broken. He took me to another ATM, where I got the same result.

I threw my hands in the air. "I don't know what else I can do," I told him. "The hotel shuttle is supposed to get here any moment. I could ask the driver to take me to an ATM."

"What hotel are you staying at?"

Should I tell him that? He would probably know by the shuttle anyway.

"Okay," he said. "I will stop by the hotel in the morning to get the money from you."

"That's fine," I told him. I wanted to put the issue to rest.

The shuttle driver was not there to meet me when I arrived. I waited alone in the dark as cab drivers and luggage handlers flooded me with offers for assistance. I told them I had no money to pay them for their services. I had only credit cards and checks, which were mostly useless in Tanzania. Most merchants, even the airlines, accepted only cash.

After what seemed like hours, my shuttle arrived. Unlike the mainland inhabitants, who usually wore Western clothing and shaved their faces, the driver donned a white kanzu and kufi and flaunted a long beard. This style of dress, I was to learn, wasn't unusual for Zanzibar, but it nonetheless perturbed me. I told the driver he would need to drop me off at an ATM, so I could get cash to pay him.

As we snaked through the dark, eerie labyrinth of Stone Town, the hairs on my neck stood on end. This was not what I expected. I had envisioned a beach resort town like Playa del Carmen in Mexico. I thought I would lounge on the beach in my bikini and loll in the Indian Ocean. Instead, silhouettes of towering derelict colonial buildings loomed over me.

Finding a working ATM proved just as tricky in Stone Town. Each time I emerged from the van, strange men scrutinized me. After trying three more ATMs, I finally found one that worked!

"Yes!" I yelled and slapped the machine. The men leered at me again.

It had taken a total of seven ATMs to find one with currency. I am not one to gamble, but I felt like I had just won at the slot machine! I got 300,000 Tanzanian shillings (about $150 US), so I wouldn't get stuck without cash again.

A few minutes later, my driver parked the shuttle van. As he gathered my luggage, he whispered, "We go this way."

I peered down the dim, narrow street that wound between the faded stone structures for which Stone Town is named.

"I don't see the hotel anywhere," I remarked.

He motioned. "It's right over here."

I froze. *Do I follow him? What if he is leading me into a trap?* I wavered in the prolonged microsecond between fear and reason. *No, this is not like what happened before. No one has ever violated me in another country.*

I followed him into the dark, cobbled alleyway—its stone walls rising from the shadows. My eyes tried to adjust to the enclosing dimness. My heart quickened, and my back tensed. My breath froze.

I must be like one of those idiots in a horror movie.

Seconds later, we arrived in front of the hotel. I dropped my shoulders and sighed as the bellman greeted me.

"Welcome to Stone Town, Miss Stuart!"

Despite the warmhearted greeting, bouts of uneasiness and vulnerability gripped me. As soon as the bellman handed over my keys, I bolted to the safety of my room.

Locking the door behind me, I collapsed on the bed, my heart still pounding. I needed to hear a familiar voice. Maybe I could talk to my best friend Heather in Texas. I tried calling her on my cell phone, only to find I had no reception. I couldn't even send a text message. What if I needed to call someone?

Terror again seized me—until I remembered I had an app on my cell phone that allowed me to call anyone in the world as if dialing from my landline. I tried to phone her again but received no answer. As a last resort, I called my mother in Oklahoma.

"Hi, honey! I am so glad to hear from you! Where are you?"

"I just made it to Zanzibar."

"Who is there with you?"

"It's just me. This wasn't a part of the tour. I just wanted to go."

"You're alone? You didn't tell me that! Where are you staying?"

"At a really nice hotel."

"Oh, honey, I wish you didn't do that. Just come home."

"I just got here. I'll be here only three days. Then I'll fly home."

"Oh, I wish you hadn't gone alone."

"I'm fine," I tried to assure her. I didn't want her to know how frightened I was.

Darn it, Mom, this is not making me feel better.

"Okay, call me tomorrow, and be careful!"

"I will."

"I love you."

"I love you, too."

* * *

WHEN I WOKE UP THE following day, I drew the curtains and was delighted to glimpse the bright blue sky and the sapphire waters of the Indian Ocean. *Maybe this place isn't so scary after all.* After pulling on my capris and tank top, I went to the lobby to plan my activities for the day. *Wouldn't it be funny if I see the skycap,* I mused.

"Good morning!" he said. I'll be darned, there he was!

"Jambo," I said, which means "Hello" in Swahili. I tried to stifle my laugh as I handed him the cash I owed for the luggage. *Unbelievable.*

"Thank you," he said. "Have a nice stay!"

He didn't give me a receipt, so I have no idea if he turned over the cash to the airline. I was to fly back to the US on a different airline, so either way, I was off the hook!

That morning, I met Newman, who took me on a tour of the historic slave market. My jaw dropped as he led me through the dark, cramped spaces where conquerors packed enslaved people before transporting them to their colonies. A few inches shorter than me, Newman didn't have to crouch as low as I did to wriggle through the drafty corridors. As he regaled me with the stories, he smiled as if he were showing me an art museum. I, on the other hand, recoiled in horror. *How could anyone treat other human beings like that?* I wondered how Newman could lead the tour, knowing what happened to his people. Perhaps he had surveyed the structure so often it didn't affect him.

As we wandered through the narrow streets of Zanzibar, some of the local women studied me. Unlike western mainland Tanzania, which is predominantly Christian, eastern Tanzania and Zanzibar are primarily Muslim. I had been to Morocco a couple of times, and the women there wore Western or traditional clothing, covering only their hair with exquisite scarves, much like my Muslim friends do in the United States.

Zanzibar was far more conservative. Most of the women here were covered head-to-toe in black burqas, only their eyes visible. I smiled and nodded at them. As sweat poured down my face, I couldn't imagine wearing more than the blue and white tank top I had on.

"What are all the religions the locals belong to?" I asked Newman.

"Most are Muslim, but we have a lot of Christians and Hindus and some Zoroastrians, too," he said. "Everyone gets along well."

As a person who is open to different worldviews and cultures, I was encouraged to hear that.

Continuing down the pinched pathways, we passed grand whitewashed façades of historic colonial buildings, most of them adorned with intricate hand-carved wooden doors, studded with conical brass spikes and door knockers. Malnourished stray cats basked in the shafts of sunlight along hidden alleyways. The cloying perfume of the frangipani trees and the smell of pungent spices, dried fish, and garlic filled the air.

As we veered around a corner, Newman took me past Freddie Mercury's childhood home, a vintage apartment building with a mahogany door and window displays that honored the famed singer. As a fan of the rock band Queen, I was excited to see Freddie's birth home! Many people don't know that the Queen frontman was born in Zanzibar and lived his first few years there. With the release of the biopic *Bohemian Rhapsody* the following year, I loved telling people I visited Freddie's birth home!

***

MY MIND RETURNED TO THE boat, where I fidgeted in my seat. *My mother would be so pissed right now*. Here I was, not knowing where I was going, to a place with no cell phone reception, alone with two men I didn't know to a deserted nineteenth-century prison.

I shuddered, recalling the last time I was alone with two males—when *It* happened—the chain of events that forever changed me. *What should I do? Dive in open water and swim back to the shore?* No, I was too far out. I had no choice but to remain onboard.

As I gazed out at the vast ocean, I beheld the light turquoise water and surging white caps of the waves. I felt the glorious warmth of the sun and the soothing ocean breeze caressing my skin. I thought, *Hollie, didn't you want an adventure? Here you have it!* At that moment, I released the tension in my body. I laughed as I thought of the irony. Here I was, worrying I would get assaulted or killed when, just six months prior, I was so depressed I wanted to die.

Part One

RISE OF THE RUNNER

CHAPTER 1

Home

Pawhuska, Oklahoma
June 2018

I SAT ON THE SECOND-FLOOR balcony of the Pioneer Woman Boarding House, gripping a cold glass of sparkling water. The hot wind that had swept through town all day finally exhausted itself and fell quiet, the night air now stifling and warm. Dimly lit by the waning moon, the rest of the town had gone to sleep. No storefronts illuminated the scene, and no cars cruised down Main Street of the charming turn-of-the-century downtown.

I had convinced my mother to take a mother-daughter trip with me. "The Boarding House is booked up two years in advance," I told her. "I was lucky to find a last-minute cancelation for one night in the Emerald Room. Come with me! It'll be fun!"

It was my hometown, the place I had lived the first nine years of my life. I marveled at how my once unknown town had become a tourist attraction, thanks to the presence of the Pioneer Woman Ree Drummond and the local production of feature films, including *August: Osage County* and the forthcoming *Killers of the Flower Moon*. It still astounds me to see photos of movie stars strolling down the timeworn streets I knew so well as a child. The streets that seem surreal because it's like a part of me never left. The streets that still pervade my dreams.

It always moves me to come back here. I have traveled all over the world, but this is the only place that evokes one word: *Home.* It's where my heart remains, and memories of my enchanting childhood linger like a half-forgotten dream. It is the one place I can go to touch the memories of my long-deceased father. I feel joyful and at peace, but also an unfulfilled longing I can never quite satisfy—of a life I lived long ago and will never live again.

Just catty-corner from me is the First National Bank, founded by my great uncle, where my dad served as vice president for several years. And across the street from the bank is where part of the Duncan Hotel, built in 1910, used to stand, now a parking lot. I remember when half of the hotel burned down. The flames grazed the east wall of the bank, where my dad's office was.

After gulping my glass of water, I tiptoed back to the Emerald Room, where my sweet mother was already asleep, and climbed into the plush mahogany bed beside her. I hadn't slept in the same bed with her since I was young. Now in her mid-seventies, she lay on her side, her hands tucked under her pillow, her chest rising and falling with each breath. I ran my fingers through her fine silver hair that glistened in front of the moonlit window. I had no idea until she later told me it made her sad to come back to Pawhuska. For me, it was a way to connect with memories of my father and the blissful remembrances of my childhood. For my mother, it was a forlorn reminder of the husband she lost and the life she left behind. As a young woman, she couldn't have imagined she would become widowed at thirty-nine with four children. I gazed at her, and my heart filled with love and gratitude. She hadn't had an easy life. She did what she needed to care for my two brothers, my sister, and me. I touched her back, glad to have her with me in the place I call home. Lulled by the clock's ticking, I lay my head on my pillow and drifted off to sleep.

* * *

I FOUND MYSELF ACROSS THE street at the bank, where my dad worked. He was forty-one years old, the age he was when he passed. I slinked in, my current age of forty-three, hoping to surprise him. Hearing my footsteps, Dad whipped around.

"There's my HoHo!" he said, flashing me his signature grin. "I am so happy to see you!"

Dad still had the same shimmering blue eyes, dark wavy hair, and handsome angular face.

"Me first!" I beamed.

That's what I always said to him as a girl. I wanted to make sure he hugged me before my siblings. Now it was a long-running quip between us.

Dad laughed and embraced me. Now that he and I were almost the same height and age, I no longer had to jump into his arms. As I gripped his slender but sturdy frame, I caught a hint of his warm, musky Old Spice cologne, a scent I had long buried in the maze of my memories. As a child, I didn't notice his slight stature. To me, he was the biggest, strongest man in the world.

I peered out the window behind Dad's desk and knew something was wrong. I could make out the red brick façade of the Duncan Hotel, completely intact.

"Didn't that building burn down?" I asked.

"No." Dad furrowed his brow and turned toward the window. "That never happened."

"I could have sworn it did a long time ago."

* * *

MY EYES FLUTTERED OPEN TO a different reality. I was back in the Emerald Room, the long-forgotten trace of Old Spice lingering in my memory. The Duncan Hotel had been consumed by fire, and Dad had died. Even though the two events weren't related, I had imagined an alternate existence—one where my dad had lived, the Duncan Hotel hadn't burned down, and we had remained in Pawhuska.

Still lying in bed, I turned to my mother, who was singing in front of the polished emerald vanity, styling her hair.

"Mom, when did the Duncan Hotel burn down?" I asked.

"Good morning, honey. Do you remember that? You were just a little girl. Your dad said that place was a fire trap."

Later, I looked up the year it burned down: 1981. I was six years old. Yes, I did remember it. Only two years later, the brief life I had known would vanish. We would lay my father to rest and say goodbye to Pawhuska, the only home I had ever known.

My mind drifted back to 1984, the year we left Pawhuska. As my mother drove off with me and my three siblings, I turned to the shrinking view of Pawhuska, the sum of my world, and felt a coil trying to draw me back. Yet, the countryside continued to roll past, a jostling portrait of the world I knew, to a place I had been, but didn't know.

The girl I was before had been whole and happy. She had no idea of the extraordinary life that lay ahead of her. She never dreamed of living outside of Pawhuska. Or of life without her father. Or of any of the losses and traumas that would befall her.

CHAPTER 2

Alternate Universe

Oklahoma City
1984 – 1988

I*T'S STILL HARD FOR ME to believe Dad is gone,* I mused to my nine-year-old self. It had been nine months since Dad died, and I found myself in a sea of strangers in an unfamiliar world, living in an alternate universe of a life that wasn't mine.

We had visited my mom's family in Oklahoma City while I was living in Pawhuska, so the city itself was not new to me. Part of me was even excited to see my grandparents, aunts, and uncles more often. However, it was altogether different to live there.

The stoplights, traffic, and bustling streets clashed with the slow, soothing pace of Pawhuska, and I longed to be in my hometown with my friends. I missed lying in the tall grass, the last rays of the sun tinting the Osage Hills in gold. I missed exploring the remote, rural areas of Osage County with my dad and climbing the sandstone bluffs near his oil leases. I missed roaming the fields and exploring the nearby woodlands, looking for unique, colorful rocks. I missed reveling in the serene beauty of the swaying bluestem grass and tranquil ponds. Would I ever find such peace and splendor again?

* * *

DURING OUR FIRST SUMMER IN Oklahoma City, I spent my days at the nearby recreation center while Mom worked at her new job. I didn't like my mom working, even though I knew it was necessary. I longed to have her by my side, just like I did as a little girl.

Unable to sleep one night, I ambled into the kitchen of our new place, the house that had not yet become home, and poured myself a glass of water. Mom must have heard me and came in. I didn't know it then, but she was young—only forty. Gray had not yet crept into her neck-length brunette hair she wore in soft curls.

"Honey, it's time to go to bed," she said.

"Mama, are you going to die?"

"Oh, no, sweetie."

"Do you promise?"

"Yes, I promise." Mom squeezed me.

How could my mom make a pledge like that? She may have reasoned it was unlikely she would die anytime soon, and it was better to reassure me. Still, I was afraid of losing her and slept with her every night for the first year after we moved.

And after Dad died, I needed her more than ever.

* * *

SCHOOL WAS ALSO A DIFFICULT adjustment. In all my subsequent years of visiting various cultures around the world, no acculturation was greater than transferring from a small-town public school to a big-city Catholic school. My mother had attended Oklahoma City Catholic schools growing up, replete with rigorous education standards and knuckle-cracking nuns. She thought her experience was so enriching she wanted her children to benefit from it, too. Maybe not so much the ill-tempered nuns, but certainly the first-rate education.

At least at Catholic school, I didn't have to worry about getting paddled or having my knuckles rapped by a ruler, but in many ways, it was stricter than Pawhuska schools. I had to wear the signature plaid jumper, which my tomboy self despised, and I was required to do something called "homework." I don't recall ever taking schoolwork home in Pawhuska.

Moreover, with my free-spirited nature, I did not fit in well. My interesting eccentricities, which made me charming and likable in Pawhuska, were almost my undoing in my oppressively conventional new school. Wearing quirky hats? Not cool. Sporting Pawhuska Husky apparel? Definitely not cool. I longed for the comfort and ease of belonging to return to me.

Making new friends was also challenging. My grade had only twenty kids, and we could fit in one classroom. Oddly, my choice of potential friends was smaller than it had been in Pawhuska. Except for a few close girl friends, all my friends in Pawhuska were boys, and they had been my friends since preschool. Ironically, in Catholic school, I didn't click with the boys in my class. Instead, most of them derided me for my Pawhuska upbringing, mocking my small-town Okie drawl—not realizing they sounded almost as Okie as I did. Loneliness—an emotion I had never felt before—filled me, and I wondered if I would find new friends. Most of the students in my class already knew each other. During recess, I withdrew into myself and walked around the playground, yearning to be back home in Pawhuska.

One day I broke the ice. I observed Laura, who had attended Catholic school since the first grade, sitting with quiet intensity by the classroom window. Unpretentious with chestnut hair styled in a bob cut, she seemed safe to approach. Bookish like me, but soft-spoken, we hit it off. Soon, I started connecting with the other girls in my class.

* * *

IN THE FIFTH GRADE, I received my wish to have a guy friend. Jason lived down the street from me, where we met every day after school to play with Transformers and Legos and watch cartoons like *Robotech* and *ThunderCats*. Even better, we embarked on adventures that harked back to my Pawhuska days. We used to sneak into the condominium complex across the street from my house and enter the vast water drainage tube that wound under the complex. When we wandered deep enough into it, we had to use flashlights to see. It's hard to say how far we ventured in the subterranean tunnel, but each time we did, we proceeded to the next maintenance hole, where we could glimpse a ray of light piercing through the darkness from the surface. Both of us Indiana Jones fanatics, we pretended we had infiltrated an ancient tomb!

Best of all, I got to do all the activities I loved with Jason. I didn't like playing the clapping games the girls in my class performed or participating in Girl Scouts. The only problem was Jason was the kid who got in trouble and caused the teachers grief. For this reason, in class, we feigned that we weren't friends. The girls wouldn't understand why I was friends with the troublemaker, and the boys would have made fun of Jason for being friends with me. But when we were alone, he was kind to me. He wasn't the obnoxious kid from class who broke the rules and ridiculed everyone. They didn't know the boy I knew.

When we weren't traversing the tunnel, we used to play in a

bamboo garden in the neighboring complex, where we broke apart the bamboo and made poles to fish in the nearby creek. One day, as we fished, he said, "I have something to tell you."

Without speaking a word, he pointed to himself, crossed his arms over his heart, and pointed to me. "I love you," he told me in sign language.

I blushed. I didn't know what to say.

The innocence of our friendship soon deteriorated, however. We started sex education in the fifth grade, and Jason became fascinated with all matters regarding sex. It was all he wanted to discuss.

Jason took me into his parents' bedroom and showed me pornographic pictures from his father's *Penthouse* and *Hustler* magazines. I flinched; I just wanted to talk about *Robotech* and *Transformers*. I hadn't even started puberty, and sex still seemed strange and gross to me.

To top it off, he had his younger sister tell me he wanted to "fuck" me. I was alarmed—I barely knew what that meant, and I tried to laugh it off. I was eleven and did not yet have a romantic interest in boys, much less have a sexual attraction to them.

One afternoon, we climbed into the boat parked by the side of his house to pretend we were seafaring.

Jason whipped around and said, "I can't wait anymore."

He pinned me down and tried to kiss me. I jerked my head from side to side to avoid his lips.

"Stop!" I screamed.

But he persisted. He seized my wrists and climbed on top of me. We weren't playing anymore. I tried to wrangle myself free.

"I love you," he said.

I squirmed enough to break loose and leapt out of the boat—

but he chased me all the way back to my house. I darted inside and slammed the door. My younger brother, who was only ten, not knowing anything was amiss, let Jason in. My brother laughed, probably thinking it was a joke or game. I knew it wasn't a game, though. Jason caught up with me in my backyard, tackled me, and tried to kiss me again.

"Stop! Please stop!" I cried.

Finally, he relented. He gazed at me a moment, got up, and left.

My mind didn't know how to reconcile what happened. I was confused and frightened. *How could he say he loved me and try to hurt me? How could I ever trust him again?*

I saw him the following day at school, where we sat in awkward silence. Wednesday. It happened on a Wednesday. Why I clung to that detail, I am not sure. I knew only that I no longer felt safe with him and tried to avoid him. In response, he taunted me in class and cast me cold stares.

Our parents wondered why we weren't friends anymore, and I never told them. Boys had always been my friends, but no more. I sealed the incident away in the recesses of my mind and had no way of knowing it would portend worse moments to come.

* * *

AFTER THE INCIDENT WITH JASON, I spent more time with the girls in my class. Most of them partook in Girl Scouts or played basketball and softball. I tried all these activities, but didn't enjoy them.

When spring arrived, the school assembled a track team. Now we were talking! I had always loved to run, even though I had never engaged in running as a sport. When I was eight years old, still in Pawhuska, the physical education teacher instructed my class to run as many laps as possible in thirty minutes. I ran ten laps, two and a half miles. While most of the kids viewed it as a punishment, I relished it. I could have run farther if he had asked. When the teacher asked each of us how far we had run, I told him I had completed ten laps.

"No, you didn't! You ran eight!" he roared. "You didn't run as far as the boys!"

I sure as heck did. I don't know how he thought he could count the laps of over twenty kids simultaneously, but he was also the football coach and much larger than me, so I thought it was better not to argue with him.

In the fourth grade, in Oklahoma City, the track coach put me in the two-hundred-meter dash, a sprint halfway around the track. At the city's Catholic Grade School Track Meet, which joined runners from all the city's Catholic schools, I placed third in the event. Not bad, but I wanted to do better.

It wasn't until sixth grade that I discovered my secret. That year, the school hosted its first Fun Run, where we had to finish as many quarter-mile laps as we could in one hour. I took off in my purple sweatsuit and sneakers, blazing laps around the school's softball and soccer fields. Running twenty-eight laps—about seven miles— and capturing first place for the whole school, I won my first trophy!

It was then I had my epiphany.

I was a long-distance runner, not a sprinter! No wonder I was mediocre in the two-hundred-meter! From that point on, I resolved to run only the eight-hundred-meter and the sixteen-hundred-meter for the Catholic school track meet. I performed much better in those events, usually placing first or second with little training. My track coach told me I was a "natural" long-distance runner.

* * *

IN ADDITION TO RUNNING, I cultivated interests that had riveted me for most of my young life. Reading was my home, my refuge, and I would lose myself in any book that awakened my curiosity and captured my imagination.

Ever since I learned to read in the first grade, I have read zealously. I loved fiction, especially novels from the Nancy Drew, Three Investigators, and Choose Your Own Adventure series. I also delighted in non-fiction, perusing books on history, astronomy, and geology.

Often my fiction reading sparked my intellectual interests. One Choose Your Own Adventure book that engrossed me was *The Mystery of the Maya*. With an all-encompassing curiosity, I became obsessed with the Maya, studying everything I could about them. The Mayans were one of the most advanced ancient civilizations, incorporating the use of zero—which was oddly uncommon in the second century A.D.—and creating a complex calendar system based on 365 days. I wondered what became of the Mayan civilization and dreamed of visiting the ruins in Central America one day.

I also read the Race Against Time series, in which Stephen, a New York teen, and his Uncle Richard travel all over the world—Morocco, Scotland, and Japan—going on exciting adventures. How cool it would be to travel the world!

In particular, I had been intrigued with Africa since my early childhood. So, in the seventh grade, I wrote a research paper on Mount Kilimanjaro. I thought the name sounded mystical, like something otherworldly. Perhaps I was also enchanted by the lyrics of the song "Africa" by the band Toto. In any case, I knew I wanted to go there someday.

Thoughts of traveling the world eased the agony of leaving Pawhuska. As painful as it was to get wrenched away from there, I realized early on I had the heart of an explorer. Pawhuska is the capital of the Osage Nation, where Osage customs are woven into nearly every part of the culture. Although I am not indigenous, the traditions captivated me. I will never forget the Osage coming to my home in their regalia shortly after my father died and performing a traditional ceremony for me and my family.

Whether it was attending the powwows or roaming the remote rural areas of Oklahoma and Kansas with my father, the lure of visiting different cultures and places enthralled me. Moving to Oklahoma City made my world even larger, and I had no idea how big it would become.

Yet as a child, I seldom traveled. My mother was a homebody, content not to leave Oklahoma City most of the time. As a result, we usually visited exotic locations like Pawhuska or Temple, Oklahoma, to see my relatives.

* * *

IN ADDITION TO VISITING OTHER cultures, the idea of visiting other worlds and different times riveted me. The space probes *Voyager 1* and *Voyager 2*, which had been launched in the '70s, were traversing the outer planets in the solar system in the '80s, transmitting a flood of information back to Earth. As a *Star Trek* enthusiast, I found that the *Voyagers'* missions seemed to fulfill the ideal that humans would one day be able to explore the universe.

Of course, my interest in science expanded into science fiction. As a ten-year-old, I went to see *Back to the Future* at the local movie theater. After watching the film, I was transfixed by the concept of altering past events. *What if I could go back in time to see my dad? Better yet, what if I could stop him from dying, like Marty McFly did with Doc Brown?*

I became fixated on movies about time travel and viewed each one I could get my hands on. I watched the 1960 classic *The Time Machine* ad nauseam, even though the lead character George travels into the distant future, not the past. I was riveted by the story's depiction of the devolution of human civilization and George's attempts to rescue it from its dystopian future. I was also captivated by the 1980 film *Somewhere in Time*, starring Christopher Reeve and Jane Seymour. In this story, Richard Collier, played by Reeve, hypnotizes himself to travel back in time from 1980 to 1912, where he meets his true love Elise McKenna, played by Seymour. While the story ends tragically, it didn't deter me from trying the experiment. I thought, *Wouldn't it be great to go back and see Dad?*

I didn't know how I would hypnotize myself to a different time and place—such as from Oklahoma City to Pawhuska—but I was willing to try. Once, I lay in bed and attempted to will my mind into thinking it was 1983 in Pawhuska when I was eight years old—right before Dad died. *What was I doing that night, anyway? Maybe I could stop Dad from driving to his oil lease.*

Try as I may, I couldn't remember the night my dad died. It's the morning after that is seared into my memory. My mother woke me up sobbing and said, "Your daddy's been killed in a car wreck." My eight-year-old mind couldn't grasp what I had just heard. I was in a state of shock and disbelief. *How could my daddy be gone?*

Back in Oklahoma City, I wondered if I could revisit that fissure in time and stop the chain of events it set in motion.

As I discovered, I couldn't.

* * *

ON THE CONTRARY, AS TIME passed, I felt my father's presence in our lives fading like an old photograph. During that period, I was aware of a breeze of tension at home that grew into a full gale whenever my sister and mother were in the same room. Kelley, my sister who was six years older than me, went into full-on rebellion. My mother couldn't control her. I imagine the trauma of Dad's death was too much for Kelley to bear. Whenever Mom and Kelley fought, I felt a sadness so pure that it bordered on despair. I usually retreated to my room or somewhere outside to escape the mayhem. If only I could bring back my father, I could restore harmony to my family.

It turned out another man would become part of our lives. When I was ten, my mom started dating John, another stark reminder that my dad was gone—for good. The brother of one of Mom's childhood friends, John had known my mother most of his life, yet I didn't meet him until we moved to Oklahoma City.

Not knowing Mom had invited him to our house, I walked into her room to tell on my sister. "Mom, Kelley farted!"

"Honey, this is my friend John," she said.

"Oh, hi," I said, peering at the man with a scraggly beard, wearing glasses and overalls.

John muttered, "Hello," and nodded at me.

At least he knew what he was signing up for if he continued to date my mother.

A longtime bachelor, farmer, and rancher, John was quiet to people who didn't know him. Once he became comfortable with someone, however, his voice boomed, and he let out hearty, belly-aching laughs that reverberated throughout the whole house. A Vietnam combat veteran, he preferred a tranquil, subdued environment, something he seldom experienced in a house with four children.

"Turn off that Dead Leopard!" he said.

"It's Def Leppard," I told him. "And it's good music!"

"Humph!" he said and stomped out of the living room.

If the noise overwhelmed him, he sometimes retreated to his farm for a few days, where he tended to his crops and livestock. As soon as he left, we cranked up the stereo. It was freedom for all of us!

Mom and John were obviously in love, and I knew it was only a matter of time before they got married. While John was simple, humble, and honest, I resented his presence. I didn't like him taking my mother's attention from me, and I wasn't ready to accept anyone else as my father. Subsequently, it took time for me to connect with him, and my hope of going back in time to reclaim my father all but vanished.

* * *

EVEN THOUGH I COULDN'T TRAVEL to different times, I got to travel to different places, thanks to my maternal grandmother Jane Thompson. Always dressed at the crest of the latest fashion, ash-gray hair styled perfectly in short, tight curls, Grandma was so worldly to me. A classy, vivacious, and forward-thinking woman, one never knew what would come out of her mouth. When I was twelve years old, she took me on a trip to Angel Fire, New Mexico, a ski resort town, to visit my Aunt DiDi, who lived there. I marveled at Grandma's poise and the deft way she navigated through the airport. I wondered if I could ever do that.

"You are about to become a teenager, and you will soon start ignoring me," she said. "That's why I want to take you on this trip."

"I will never do that," I assured her.

It was my first time flying on a commercial jet and the first flight I had taken since I was about eight years old. My dad, a licensed pilot, used to fly my family and me in my grandfather Stuart's Cessna to various locales in Oklahoma. However, the Cessna could not reach thirty thousand feet like a commercial jet. I leaned my forehead against the window, admiring the medley of landmarks and topography below.

As Grandma and I descended into New Mexico, sunlight spilled over the peaks and illumined the majestic landscape. I had never viewed mountains from the air, and I was entranced to view the world from such an ethereal place.

When we arrived in Angel Fire, my aunt and uncle greeted us at the small local airport. I gaped at the ice-blue sky, snow-covered peaks, and verdant conifers. I inhaled the crisp mountain air.

"What would you like to do?" Aunt DiDi asked.

"I want to go exploring!" I said.

"I know just where to take you."

Bundled up in our winter gear, DiDi took me hiking through the forest near her property. I was mesmerized by the sublime beauty of the mountains and trees, which reminded me so much of the Osage Hills. With snow blanketing the ground, however, I could not search for interesting rocks. To satisfy my curiosity, she drove me to Cimarron, a nearby village with a rock and mineral store, where I selected several local specimens to add to my rock collection.

Angel Fire is also where I tried snow-skiing for the first time. I was so confident after a few lessons; I was ready to tackle one of the blue-rated declines. My aunt, of course, reined me in and told me to stick with the green-rated runs. Sure enough, on my last day there, I grazed down the green slope, headed toward the lodge, and lost control of my skis. Crashing face-first into the snow, my sunglasses shattered on my face, casting off a cloud of powdery white flurries. Despite mild bruising, I bounced up, ready to take on the next slope!

The ski crash wasn't the only memorable event. The next day when we departed for Oklahoma City, a major blizzard struck Angel Fire right after takeoff. As we ascended, nothing but opaque whiteness colored the world outside. The plane pitched, and I found myself plastered against the window. Each time the small jet lurched, I felt my stomach flipflop. I cast a frightened look at Grandma.

"Don't worry," she said. "You have a white light around you. You're safe."

Just in case, I braced myself, grasping the seat in front of me. After an hour of turbulence, we cleared the storm. The plane descended and flared to a touchdown over the shimmering asphalt, squealing its tires and tearing down the runway.

When the plane stopped, I exhaled the breath I didn't realize I had been holding. That was close!

When we disembarked the plane, I asked Grandma, "Weren't you scared?"

"I was scared to death, but had to act brave for you."

"What about the white light you talked about?"

"It was there protecting us, and we made it here safely," she said.

Thirty years later, Grandma's white light would save me again.

CHAPTER 3

Sex, Guys, and Catholic School

Oklahoma City
1987 – 1988

DESPITE THE HARDSHIPS OF ADJUSTING to Catholic school, I began adapting, and my natural silliness shone through again. While I was mostly well-behaved, my humor and jokes often straddled the line. Because the culture was stifling for me, I felt the need to push the boundaries and keep my teachers on their toes.

Sometimes, it was more fun to *look like* I was breaking the teachers' rules. When we were in eighth grade, the school allowed us to have a "beach day," for which we got to wear beach clothes, instead of our uniforms, and bring our blankets and boom boxes with us on the playground. The teachers told us not to play any "inappropriate" music. With my boom box in hand, I blared Mötley Crüe's hit, "Shout at the Devil."

"Hollie, is that song saying something about the devil?" Mrs. Morgan asked. A genteel woman in her fifties, I imagine she didn't listen to heavy metal.

"Yeah, it's saying to shout at him." I giggled.

"I don't think that sounds appropriate," she said.

"Well, they are shouting at him to go away," I said.

"Hollie, you are something else," she said as she shook her head and walked off.

My friend Laura lamented, "It's not fair. You break the teachers' rules, and they still love you."

"They know I'm kidding," I told her. "They think I am funny, but have to act like they're mad."

* * *

WHEN I WAS TWELVE YEARS old, I ran my own "publication," for which I wrote humorous sketches and caricatures, often involving members of my family and friends. No one in my circle was free from getting roasted, but my mom, aunts, grandma, and older brother provided the most fruitful material. I often inserted them in absurd situations, lampooning all their character traits. My mother has only a couple of my writings left, and it's interesting to see how my young mind took everyday people and situations and satirized them.

I often found opportunities for jokes in school as well. In the seventh grade, Mrs. Angelo, a kind, prim woman in her fifties, showed us how companies use sex to promote their products. Shifting her reading glasses from her short brunette hair down to her narrow face, she held up a Fab detergent advertisement, which depicted a shirtless man in tight jeans. She said Fab had no reason to use that image. She also presented us with a perfume ad that flaunted a woman wearing a sheer, loosely-draped shawl, exposing "excessive skin."

A couple of months later, during the summer, Laura and I devised a plan to mail Mrs. Angelo innocent-looking magazine ads, accusing the advertisers of using sex to promote their products. I could imagine the total look of confusion on Mrs. Angelo's face. I drafted a handwritten letter, which Laura used to type a formal notice:

> *Dear Mrs. Angelo,*
>
> *Can you believe this? These ads are using SEX to advertise their products! Shame on them! I highly recommend you write a letter of complaint to each of these companies. If they don't stop this type of advertising, sue them and settle this thing in court!*
>
> *Signed,*
> *People who are taking charge*
>
> *P.S. Did you complain to Fab?*

We looked up Mrs. Angelo's address in the phone directory and enclosed some innocuous ads in an envelope to mail her. One was for A.1. Steak Sauce, which depicted a plate of barbecue.

When we returned to school later that summer, I eagerly awaited Mrs. Angelo's reaction. "Hi, Mrs. Angelo! Did you get a letter over the summer?"

Mrs. Angelo smirked. "You're the one who sent that. I should have known it was you." She added, "I didn't know what I was supposed to look for."

I cackled. "It's whatever you want to see!"

Fortunately, Mrs. Angelo was good-natured and thought it was funny.

***

WHEN WE STARTED SEVENTH GRADE, the teachers began discussing sexual morality with us, using ridiculous '70s textbooks with pictures that could have been mistaken for scenes from *The Brady Bunch* or *The Partridge Family*. They told us, of course, not to have sex before we were married, as it was a sin. Not only that, but no "heavy petting" or "deep" kissing until we were married, according to Mrs. Angelo. *Heavy petting?* I had petted my dog, but that was about it. *Do people do that to each other? And deep kissing? That's a new one.*

One student in the class asked what all of us were thinking: "What is deep kissing?"

Mrs. Angelo replied, "You know, French kissing."

The class uttered a simultaneous, "Ohhhh . . ." and snickered.

If the teachers were going to talk about sex with teenagers, they could at least dispense with the laughable '70s textbooks and avoid antiquated terms. But I guess that's what happens when most of your teachers are in their fifties.

Looking back on it now, after everything that has happened, I wonder why the school was so fixated on maintaining "chastity" and abstinence. On one hand, presenting the risks of having sex made perfect sense. After all, it was desirable to avoid teen pregnancy, an STD, or adverse psychological repercussions. Even so, why was the school teaching only a no-tolerance policy to sex outside of marriage or the use of birth control and prophylactics, especially in the midst of the AIDS epidemic? "Just say no," they said.

They, however, overlooked one glaring omission. *What if saying "no" doesn't work?*

* * *

BY SEVENTH GRADE, ALL OF us girls had become interested in boys. We often shared the *Teen Beat* and *Big Bopper* magazines, which featured the poster boys of the day—River Phoenix, Corey Haim, Corey Feldman, Patrick Swayze, Tom Cruise, Rob Lowe, and others—and sat around at each other's houses listening to Madonna, Cyndi Lauper, Tiffany, Debbie Gibson, George Michael, Bon Jovi, and Def Leppard. Overnight, my interests shifted from rocks, Legos, and cartoons to boys and teen romance series like Sweet Valley High. I didn't know how realistic these novels were in terms of how teens interacted with each other, but they set an ideal that was far different from what I experienced. Moreover, I had been a tomboy for most of my life, and boys had been my buddies, not potential romantic partners. Out of nowhere, I was concerned with how appealing I was to boys my age and didn't know how to relate to them. If only my sister were there, she could teach me. Unlike me, Kelley was blonde, sexy, stylish, and could flirt effortlessly. However, she had left home two years earlier, and I seldom saw her.

For my thirteenth birthday, I invited the girls over to watch *Dirty Dancing*, which had been released that year. We kept rewinding the scene on the VCR where Patrick Swayze gets out of bed, and we swooned each time.

"You know this is wrong, don't you?" said Mom, referring to the bedroom scenes.

"Yeah, Mom," I said, just to agree with her. But we didn't quit watching it, and she didn't tell us to stop the movie.

At my sleepover, I discovered that John, now my stepfather, had a higher tolerance for boisterous girls than boys. My girlfriends and I stayed up all night talking and giggling, but he didn't say a word. If my brothers and their friends, on the other hand, made a peep, he sometimes snapped at them to be quiet. I asked John why he didn't like teenage boys. He said, "Because they are ugly and stupid." Enough said.

* * *

AS FUN AS SEVENTH GRADE had been, any good cheer ceased right before my eighth-grade year. My blood pressure has always run low, making it difficult for me to wake up. One morning, I jumped straight from bed into the shower. As the hot water poured over me, I lost consciousness. The next thing I knew, I was lying on the bathroom floor, where I heard my mother screaming. My chin had busted open where I hit the tile, and the sides of my face throbbed. Everything was a blur. I faded in and out, my mother panicking and crying.

Mom rushed me to the emergency room, where the staff ran an X-ray on me. I had broken my jaws. My mother started sobbing, and I didn't know what that meant for me.

I was admitted to the hospital, where a surgeon wired my mouth shut so the bones could mend. I stayed two nights in the hospital with Mom and John by my side. I was especially touched when John stayed overnight, sleeping in my room's stiff, upright chair. Maybe he wasn't my dad, but I could tell he loved me, and I couldn't help but feel love for him.

That meant I had to start school with my mouth wired, unable to speak or eat, and go on a liquid diet for nourishment. For a thirteen-year-old girl, it was a major blow to my self-esteem. Most everyone in my class was understanding, but it was difficult not to be able to express myself. Hanging out with my girlfriends on the playground, I couldn't engage in conversation.

It seemed like months before I had the wires cut. I was delighted when my doctor told me I could go on a soft-food diet for a month! Mom, Grandma, and I celebrated with a delightful meal at the Olive Garden. I hadn't tasted real food for so long! I savored the lasagna and breadsticks, grateful I could ingest solid food again. However, I didn't know my gums would grow over my teeth due to lack of use, and I had to wait for them to recede. As a result, when I went to school events or football games and met cute boys, I felt mortified and unsightly. It would take another month before I could regain full use of my speech and eat without restriction, leaving an awkward imprint on my confidence.

* * *

BREAKING MY JAWS WAS JUST the beginning of the trauma I experienced that year. Thanks to my brothers, we had the house in the neighborhood to which all the kids flocked. It seemed like we had a constant stream of boys coming over to hang out, play basketball, and watch TV. Usually, my mother was there, and all our friends adored her. When my younger brother and I became teenagers, we had a couple of hours to ourselves most days between the time we came home from school to when Mom arrived home from work. When the neighborhood boys came over, they mostly left me alone while they played basketball outside.

Because the influx of boys at my house was so common, one incident caught me off-guard. When I was thirteen—sometime in November 1988—I went into the kitchen to get a snack. Two of the neighborhood boys who were around my age came in there. Without any warning, the boys grabbed my breasts. I was stunned! No one had ever touched me there before.

I jumped back and yelled, "Hey, don't do that!"

Both boys bellowed, thinking they had pulled off something hilarious. I had known these boys for years, and they had never behaved that way before.

What progressed over the next two months does not play like a continuous reel in my mind. It's more like a horror movie—in which frames are missing or skipped over—or like a shattered mirror, where I discern certain fragments, but struggle to place all the pieces together logically or temporally. Soon after the incident in my kitchen, the boys came over again, cornered me, and grabbed my private parts.

Something unexpected stirred inside of me—a tiny swell of sensuality, a force not yet fully awake. Part of me was curious about this new sensation. Another part of me told me how wrong it was, the shame swallowing me. I was not sexually or emotionally attracted to these boys—disgusted by them, rather—and I didn't understand how I could have a physical reaction to their marauding touch.

Exactly how many times this happened, I don't recall. My memories are disjointed, like a broken kaleidoscope. All I know is I wanted it to stop, but each time it happened, I felt like I lost a piece of myself and became further consumed by my shame. I was no longer a girl. I was a body, an object for them to use as they pleased.

I tried to no avail to get the boys to stop. I told them "no"—just like I had been taught.

Soon I retreated into my shell, seldom talking to anyone. I quit doing much of my schoolwork, and my grades plummeted. My teachers, who had always known me as a bright, silly, quirky student, didn't know what had happened to me.

As much as I tried for many years to forget these incidents, the next scene has always loomed large in my mind, as the memory I cannot erase. The next time the boys came over, in what would have been December, I confronted them.

"Leave me alone! I don't want you to touch me!"

They just laughed and lunged toward me. I ran off, but Boy #1 caught me by my shirt. As I tried to pull away, my blouse tore down the seam. Both boys pinned me down in my family's living room. They ripped my blouse, skirt, bra, and underwear off. Boy #2 held me down while Boy #1 forced himself on me. They traded places. Boy #1 held me down, while Boy #2 followed suit.

"Stop, please stop!" I screamed.

They continued their attack. Boy #1 laughed. He was the aggressor.

I squirmed and tried to wrench myself free—but I couldn't overtake both of them. After the boys had had enough, they finally ended their assault on me. I lay on the floor in my living room, my ripped uniform blouse and skirt next to me. A million thoughts cascaded through my mind. *What do I do with these? How will I explain this to my mother? No, I can't. I have to throw them away. Am I still a virgin? If I'm not, I am a really bad person. No, I'm not just bad; I am terrible. I am a sinner. My teachers and my family would be so ashamed of me. I am ugly. I am nothing.*

I buried my face in the carpet and cried of overwhelming guilt and shame, of a pain too deep to be verbalized, except in the language of choked tears.

CHAPTER 4
Lost Soul

Oklahoma City
December 1988

IN THE COMING WEEKS, THE trees shed their leaves, and the dark gray skies augmented the agony brought on by the worst days of my life. I was only a semblance of my former self. Where I used to be quick and funny, I was now duller, as if my insides looked just as bleak as winter outside. A cloud of lethargy loomed over me, and I wandered around in a daze, searching for something I had lost. I still looked like me, but the Hollie everyone knew was gone. It took everything for me to get out of bed in the morning. I had ceased doing most of my schoolwork and drifted throughout the day. At night, I lay in bed and wondered if it would be better to fall asleep and never wake up. I wasn't worthy of anything good—love, friendship, respect.

That year, our class played Secret Santa, and one of the boys in the class was assigned to me. I usually sent my person candy and notes. This year, I decided to write him what I thought was a funny story. I had just read parts of the *Iliad*, so I composed an absurd anecdote about a warrior goddess named Lady Trojan who seduced the adult male characters. Humor has always been my coping mechanism. And, in a way, I was trying to find a sense of empowerment in what had occurred, or I was going to die inside.

The note was admittedly salacious and intended to shock. Even so, the boy was more alarmed than I anticipated and turned it over to the principal. I expected the story to get attention, just not the attention it did. Considering I attended a religious school, the story was taken seriously.

Somehow the letter got traced back to me, and I found myself sitting face-to-face with the principal in her office. Hands clasped on her desk, she glared at me through her large spectacles. My eyes slid down to the crumpled paper lying flat on her workspace. I gazed back up at her broad face, her forehead perspiring under her round, puffed-up hair.

She held up the piece of paper. "This is the worst note I have ever read. I am going to call your mother," she said.

I didn't respond, thinking, *No problem. My mom knows I write funny stories. She will just giggle.*

When the principal read the entire story to my mother over the phone, I about died laughing. To hear her say such risqué words tickled me.

She hung up and said, "Your mother is coming over here," to which I shrugged.

To my surprise, my mother didn't react the way I thought she would.

She charged into the office. "Where did you learn those things?" she cried.

I gaped when I saw the anger and shame etched on her face.

"I don't even know who you are anymore!" she shrieked.

I recoiled from my mother's words as if they were hot cinders spat from a fire. Staring at her in disbelief, I broke down and started bawling. The truth is I didn't know who I was, either. I only knew I was bad. Of all the people in the world I did not want to disappoint, it was her. My mother was *everything* to me.

I returned to class sobbing. *My mother is upset with me over a ridiculous note. Imagine if she knew my secret. She would be so ashamed of me.*

What she and the principal didn't know was that this incident was a cry for help, but I didn't know how to ask for it. I had to carry this heavy burden and live with the belief that I was a terrible person and deserved what had happened to me. The story I wrote was a red flag, but not the one they imagined. I was not some hypersexual teenager on the verge of promiscuity. I was a thirteen-year-old girl who was exposed to a vile world she should have been too young to know and had almost no love remaining for herself.

* * *

A COUPLE OF WEEKS LATER, I strolled past Mrs. Morgan's desk and opened one of her drawers. I found the blank geography tests and took one out.

The art teacher saw me and said, "You know, you shouldn't take things out of a teacher's desk." She told Mrs. Morgan what I had done, and Mrs. Morgan took me aside in the hall.

She whispered, "Hollie, why is it that you seem to get in nothing but trouble lately?"

I searched her face, sensing the worry in her pale blue eyes. "I don't know . . ." I said, looking away.

My eyes must have conveyed my unfathomable pain, for she whispered, "You know, I am on your side. If you ever need to talk about anything, I'm here."

I later considered what she said to me. Out of all the teachers, she was the one who had approached me with compassion. I was almost at the end of my rope and didn't know what else to do.

The next day I walked up to Mrs. Morgan and asked, "Can I talk to you?"

She smiled and said, "Yes, of course."

It was the day before Christmas break began. Mrs. Morgan took me into one of the offices. I gazed at her, wondering if I should tell her. This woman was even older than my mother, the quintessential '50s lady. She carried herself with the deportment of an old-fashioned Southern belle. Would she understand? As if reading my thoughts, she nodded.

"There are some things you don't know about me, and you might be shocked to hear them," I said.

She reassured me. "Hollie, I raised two kids. I don't think you could tell me anything that would shock me."

I took a deep breath and told her, "Some boys have been coming to my house, and they have been touching me." Just saying the words took a massive weight off me. Nonetheless, I couldn't bring myself to tell her the whole truth—that I wasn't sure if I was a virgin.

"Some guys have been harassing you? Is that why you haven't been yourself lately?"

"Yeah," I told her.

"Hollie, it's your body, and no one else is allowed to touch it." She continued, "If you want them to touch you, that's another story, but no one can touch you without your permission. That is supposed to be a sign of affection between two people, not something someone takes from you."

I thought about my body's response, and a stab of shame lanced me.

I teared up and said, "I don't know how to make them stop, and I can't tell anyone. Please don't tell my mom," I begged her. "I wrote that story, and she won't understand. She's still upset with me about it."

"I won't tell," she assured me. "What about telling a brother or sister? Can they make them stop?"

"I don't want to tell them what's happening, either," I said. I couldn't bear the shame of anyone in my family knowing.

"Somehow, it must be stopped," Mrs. Morgan said. "I am sure this is affecting your self-esteem," she added.

"Yes," I replied. *Actually, I hate myself,* I thought.

After a few seconds of silence, she said, "Nothing you have told me has shocked me. I don't think you're a bad person. I just think you have a few problems right now." She paused and asked, "Do you feel better?"

"Yes," I told her. I felt so relieved, for someone to understand me, even if I couldn't explain the full extent of what happened.

As I mulled over our conversation later, I decided Mrs. Morgan was right. I had to tell my family *something*. I couldn't go on like this anymore. What had Mrs. Morgan told me? Yes, the boys were *harassing* me. A couple of days later, I told my brother just that.

The next time the boys came over, he ordered them, "Quit messing with my sister."

At last, they quit coming over, but they had already done irreparable damage.

Christmas, which had always been a joyful, magical time of year for me, became forlorn and cheerless. Winter fell with a heaviness that deepened the hole in my heart, and I felt a million years old. I barely lumbered out of bed each morning and slept throughout the day, even during class. Consequently, some of the guys in my class began fabricating rumors that I was doing drugs. On the contrary, I was suffering from something even more insidious—severe depression.

CHAPTER 5
Acting Out

Oklahoma City
Spring 1989

I THOUGHT I WAS RUINED in my mother's eyes. A rift had opened between us, and she would never see me the same way. Telling her what happened to me was not an option. With my mother already engulfed in the lingering grief from my father's passing, the last thing I wanted was to cause my mother more pain. I needed to protect her. Plus, she was already going through so much with my sister. Kelley had become entangled with drugs, alcohol, and men. The word "alcoholic" had not yet been uttered, but it was obvious to almost everyone. Sometimes she disappeared for weeks at a time, and we worried if she was dead or alive—something that plagued my family until I was eighteen, the year my sister went into treatment. What my mom didn't know was that watching Kelley's precipitous demise made me never want to abuse alcohol or drugs.

Most of all, I was too ashamed to tell Mom what had happened to me.

During Christmas break, Mom took me to see *Mystic Pizza* at the movie theater. When a sexual encounter between two of the main characters flashed on the screen, I flinched and peered at my mother beside me. After I wrote the story, Mom said she would limit what I watched. However, she continued to gaze at the screen. Noticing no reaction, I hoped, ever so briefly, that our relationship would return to normal.

Meanwhile, I had never felt so alone. I felt disconnected from everyone, even my friends, and didn't know where I fit in or belonged. I couldn't tell anyone what had happened to me.

And nothing makes us lonelier than our secrets.

I don't think anyone knew what to make of the change in me, which further exacerbated my feelings of isolation and loneliness. I longed for people to like me, but I didn't even like or love myself anymore.

* * *

WHEN SCHOOL RESUMED, I THOUGHT maybe life would get better. I couldn't have been more mistaken.

On the way from the classroom to the lunchroom, I played tag with three of the boys. To be clever, they ran into the boys' restroom, where they thought they could elude me. I darted into the restroom after them. As soon as they saw me, one of them switched off the light. Within seconds, one of the boys grabbed my privates. I screamed in shock, bolting out of the restroom as fast as I could.

The unrelenting shame rippled through me. *Why does this keep happening?* I cried to myself. I could conclude only one explanation: I deserved it. God was punishing me. I should never have gone into the boys' bathroom.

To make matters worse, that afternoon, one of the teachers

reprimanded me for going into the boys' restroom. *How could I tell her what happened?* After all, she was right—*I shouldn't have gone in there.* Besides, I didn't know which of the three boys assaulted me.

I tried to suppress my memory of the incident, overshadowed by the occurrences from a few months before. When I try to coax the memories into clarity, I remember only one of the boys, whom I suspect violated me. The other two loom in my mind as indistinct, ghoulish figures, perhaps unwitting bystanders to what happened.

Overall, the cumulative losses of the past few years were almost more than I could endure. The loss of my father. The loss of my hometown. The loss of my sense of security, knowing I could lose a parent at any moment. The loss of my sense of safety and innocence. The loss of my friends. The loss of people's respect for me. The loss of my mother's approval. And worst of all, the loss of love for myself and who I thought I was.

Meanwhile, some of the boys also groped a couple of the girls right in front of everyone, including the teachers. The teachers told them to stop, but the boys did not, and to my knowledge, they were never disciplined. When I spoke to one of the girls about it, she said that one of the teachers said to her, "You know, you're just offering yourselves to them." When I view the situation now, I see how warped and misguided it was—blaming the girls for the boys' reprehensible behavior.

I continued to skip my homework assignments and wondered if the year would ever end. I was chronically late for class, partially due to my low blood pressure, but mostly I didn't want to face the other kids and endure the agonizing loneliness, the feeling that I was no longer a good person.

* * *

ONE AFTERNOON, WE TOOK A science test for which I had not studied. Without prior consideration, I looked up the answers to the test by opening my science book during the exam. I peered at the front of the classroom to ensure Mrs. Morgan was distracted. The next thing I knew, she sprung up behind me, snatched my book from me, slammed it closed, and wrote *0%* on my test. She was furious.

The following week, Mrs. Roberts, my English teacher, asked us to write a report on a book we were assigned to read. I had tried to study the book, but found the writing insufferable. This was noteworthy, considering I loved to read. When Mrs. Roberts asked us to write the report in class, I couldn't even recall the title of the book, much less the author. So, next to the title and the author, I wrote a question mark. For the summary, I added another question mark. Under the recommendation, I wrote, "I don't know about the book because I read only the first two pages, which were boring. If the rest of the book was like the first two pages, which it probably was, I wouldn't recommend it." *Hilarious!*

I knew I wouldn't receive a stellar grade on the book report, but I was surprised when I received zero percent. I expected to get at least a few points for my recommendation. I showed it to some of my classmates, who laughed. I did, too. Even now, I still think it's funny. Even now, I don't like boring books. Mrs. Roberts, a petite, typically mild-mannered woman in her fifties with short charcoal hair, cast me a steely look. Oops, I had pissed her off too.

After those incidents, Mrs. Morgan gave me a disciplinary referral and asked to meet with my mom and me. Mrs. Morgan and Mrs. Roberts told my mother everything I had done wrong, and that I had a "bad attitude." They said they didn't want me to feel bad; they just wanted the "old Hollie" back—the one who had been colorful, quirky, and funny. Inside, though, I had turned as gray as the clouds outside. Mrs. Roberts told me I was her best English student and best writer. Mrs. Morgan added I was one of the smartest kids in the class; I didn't need to cheat. Of course, I was acting out and wanted the adults in my life to notice me. Negative attention was better than no attention at all and seemed to reinforce my new belief that I was a bad person.

After Mom and I left, she asked me if I was okay, and I said yes. She seemed concerned, but not mad. It was my lonely rebellion, against what or whom, I didn't know.

After that meeting, I determined I didn't need my teachers on my bad side, so I put more effort into school and studied more than I normally would for my next science test. I made ninety-five percent, enough to offset the zero percent and receive a passing grade for the quarter.

* * *

LATER THAT SPRING, OUR CLASS convened for a retreat, where the teachers asked all the parents to write a letter to their children. My mother wrote me the sweetest note. The content has blurred in my memory, and I don't know what happened to it, but I remember it said, *I love you because you're you.* It was hard to believe because I didn't love myself anymore.

My only saving grace was track season starting. Having learned I was not a sprinter a couple of years before, I told my coach I wanted to run distance races. While practices were not structured, I met the rest of the team after school to run variable distances around the playground and the baseball fields. Running warmed my soul, and for a moment, I stepped outside the pain and horror of my present life and raced in my mind through the idyllic hillsides and neighborhoods of Pawhuska. I channeled all the anguish, anger, and hurt I couldn't express into my running. More than anything, racing gave me something I desperately needed—the power over my body I had lost. At the Catholic Grade School Track Meet, I won third place in the eight-hundred-meter and the sixteen-hundred-meter runs, clocking respectable times.

While running brought me joy, I continued to face reminders of the traumatic events that had occurred that year. In May, a miniseries aired on local television called *I Know My First Name Is Steven,* a true story about a seven-year-old boy who had been kidnapped and repeatedly raped by his captor. The drama both horrified and transfixed me. In particular, I recall the scene where Steven testified in court, regaling the harrowing details of the abuse, and how taxing it was for him to say the words aloud. *What happened to me wasn't anything like that. At least I wasn't abducted and attacked by a stranger, so I wasn't abused,* I reasoned.

The teachers often spoke about what to do if a stranger approached us. What they didn't tell us, or perhaps they didn't know, was that kids were not usually abused, attacked, or abducted by strangers, but by people they know and trust.

* * *

AT THE BEGINNING OF MAY, our religion teacher asked me to write the class graduation speech. I was surprised, considering I hadn't excelled academically that year, but Mrs. Roberts told her I was the best writer in the class. I basked in the praise, wondering how I could write a speech after experiencing one of the worst years of my life, a most anticlimactic ending to my grade school years.

For the speech, I had no way of seeing or projecting myself in the future. I couldn't even see beyond the month, much less through high school years and beyond. Instead, I imagined what we would be like as a group of adults one day, working and raising children just like our parents. While the speech itself was not woeful, my melancholy delivery betrayed the pain I had tried so hard to conceal. When it came time for the teachers to present the academic honors, I felt instant regret I had not done the appropriate work to receive any awards. I was capable of so much more. Despite that sentiment, when the athletic director conferred my awards for track, I felt a faint hint of hope.

The reception afterward was bittersweet. My friends and I reminisced on our shared memories and took pictures. My aunt Nancy lent me a stunning long white dress and fixed my hair in a French braid with the perfect '80s hair and makeup. It was the first time in a while I had felt beautiful.

Facing another ending, I walked out that night both relieved and terrified of leaving this period of my life behind, not knowing what would happen next.

CHAPTER 6

Rise and Run

Oklahoma City
Summer – Fall 1989

IF I THOUGHT WAKING UP at seven a.m. was a drag in grade school, waking up for cross country practice at five thirty was pure agony. My mom, ever the morning lark, knocked on my bedroom door, flipped on the light, and said, "Good morning, sunshine! Time to wake up!"

I groaned and buried my head in my pillow. It was summertime and still dark outside. *Who the hell wakes up this early?* Mom came by a couple more times to rouse me. At last, I floundered out of bed and staggered into my shorts and T-shirt.

Once I woke up, I looked forward to running for my high school cross country team. By sheer luck, my school had one of the best girls' cross country and track programs in the state, the girls just having won the state championship in track a few months earlier.

I arrived at the track to glimpse chattering silhouettes circling the dark oval. Coach, an enthusiastic man in his late thirties with slightly long, shaggy brown hair, welcomed us to the first practice. I had met him the year before when he visited my eighth-grade class to speak with us about attending high school. I was immediately taken by his warmth and exuberance. He often said, "Awesome!" before most people his age said it.

"Good morning, folks!" Coach beamed. "Let's warm up with a couple of laps!"

After a series of stretches, Coach led us on a three-mile run through the neighboring streets. By the time we returned to the track, we had just enough time to shower in the locker room and jet to class.

"Good job, girls!" Coach cheered.

When I arrived at my first class, I already felt exhausted, but the excitement of my first day of high school soon reenergized me. I found some of my grade school friends, and we kept our eye out for others in our class.

Even with the hope of beginning anew and leaving behind the painful memories from the last year, I still felt worthless and broken. But at least I didn't have to see the boys who—

My throat tightened, and I willed myself not to finish the thought.

* * *

CROSS COUNTRY MEETS DID NOT get canceled for any type of weather. With the season starting in late summer and ending in the fall, we endured everything from hundred-degree blazing heat to freezing weather and torrential downpours. While I despised rising early for practice, I enjoyed the cool, tranquil mornings of late August and the rush of fresh air filling my lungs.

For our first race, the other freshmen girls and I queued up in our portion of the starting box. Unlike track races, which amass only a few competitors, cross country races could have dozens of competitors running in an open field. To place in the top ten is considered impressive. As a freshman, I wasn't fast enough to qualify for the varsity team, which consisted of the top seven runners, so I competed in the junior varsity races with the other freshmen.

While we lingered on the starting line, clouds gathered, and the smell of impending rain permeated the atmosphere. Perhaps we wouldn't have to run in the heat after all. I felt electricity in the air, both from the anticipation of running my first high school race and the inevitable onset of the pending storm. Sure enough, sprinkles started falling and formed liquid globes on my skin. I welcomed the cool shower on what had been a scorching week.

By the time the starting gun crackled, water cascaded from the sky. As we zipped down the field, mud flung from the runners in front of me, and quasi-dry ruts transformed into deep pools. Sweat and rain soaked my eyelashes and blurred my vision. As I strode onward, the course became so waterlogged that my heel sank in the mud and suctioned my shoe like quicksand. I had two choices. Continue without my shoe or stop to retrieve it. I prodded my shoe from the muck and slipped it back on.

I had no idea how I was performing. My focus was not to get stuck and keep forging ahead. After two miles of slogging through the mud, I came upon the finish line. As I cruised through the finisher's chute, I found out I had placed seventh!

Thankfully, the extreme weather conditions didn't persist. As the season progressed, I came to love racing on the courses of earth, turf, and rolling hills. It reminded me of running out in the country on Skyline Drive in Pawhuska or dashing around my dad's oil leases in the remote parts of Osage County.

Most of all, running cross country brought me joy and confidence. It filled the massive void in my soul. While I didn't make the varsity team of the top seven runners, I continued to improve throughout the season and enjoyed competing in the junior varsity meets. Coach applauded his junior varsity athletes as ardently as he did his varsity athletes. He often shouted at me from the sideline, "Come on, Hollie, pick it up! You got this!"—even though I felt like I was dying.

At the end of the season, Coach accompanied the top ten girls and boys to the State meet. Runners 8–10 were to serve as alternates if any of the seven varsity runners couldn't compete. While I wasn't sure of my exact rank, it was an honor for me to attend the State meet as an alternate and a freshman on a state championship team. It kindled a glow I hadn't felt in some time.

Even though I didn't finish varsity that year, I ended up lettering in cross country. Overall, it was a highlight of my freshman year. At the end-of-season banquet, Coach told our supporters, "Hollie is part of our reloading. We look for her to be even better next year." I hoped he was right.

CHAPTER 7

Making a Run for It

Oklahoma City
Winter 1989 – 1990

THE CHILLING NOVEMBER AIR CAST a cold gust on the cinders of warmth I felt during the cross country season. The one pursuit that had given me comfort, self-assurance, and a sense of belonging faded with the receding daylight. On top of it all, my grade school friends had branched out and become friends with other students in our class. I lapsed into a deep depression, evocative of the one I had experienced a year before.

I leaned my head against the wall in my bedroom, closed my eyes, and tried to fight the sudden surge of pain and the flood of tears. I used to love the Christmas season, but any joy I had felt before vanished. Even worse, I had to act like I was happy, which was exhausting.

* * *

IT SEEMED LIKE MONTHS BEFORE track season started in January. Fortunately, with track practice after school, I didn't have to wake up at five thirty a.m. Unlike cross country, which consisted of single two-mile races, track presented a variety of events, ranging from the one-hundred-meter dash to the thirty-two-hundred-meter run. The question was which events to compete in.

Many people assume track and cross country are one and the same. After all, they both involve running. Not only do the course conditions of each sport differ, but the sprinters and the distance runners embody two different types of beasts. The sprinters' art revolves around a single explosive instant, in which all is gained or lost, particularly in the races that last less than one minute. The distance runners, on the other hand, are the serene messengers who perform their best surmounting wooded trails and mountain paths. They descend from the animals who test the limits of the human body and spirit. Having gone to the edge and back, they understand they will need to hurt for several minutes, sometimes hours.

I knew from running track in grade school I was not a sprinter. Even Coach told me the longer the distance, the better for me. That meant I would race in the thirty-two-hundred-meter at the junior varsity meets—eight laps around the track. I did not look forward to it.

At a meet early in the season, I was pacing myself well in the thirty-two-hundred-meter, setting myself up to place. With only two laps left, however, a peculiar sensation came over me. My body grew weaker and weaker. By the time I neared the last stretch, my legs, reduced to jelly, could hardly support me. I willed myself to stagger to the finish line. As soon as I crossed, I almost collapsed, catching myself before I hit the ground. Oddly enough, I didn't pass out or lose consciousness, like I had when I broke my jaws a year and a half before. Unlike that incident, I was still alert, but couldn't move my body.

Coach and other spectators rushed over to me.

"Get up," Coach said. "You need to stand up." He and another coach hoisted me.

"I can't," I muttered.

The coaches clasped me under my arms and pulled me forward, my toes dragging the ground.

"I don't know what happened," I droned.

"You're dehydrated," Coach said. "Here, drink some water."

He held the bottle to my mouth as he and another coach heaved me back to the camp, where the remainder of the team rested.

"Stay here and keep drinking water," Coach said. "Don't worry about running the mile."

I was scheduled to run the sixteen-hundred-meter in the afternoon, but that wouldn't happen. Utterly depleted, I recovered only well enough to walk.

"That was crazy," one of my teammates said. "Your eyes were popping out of your head on the last stretch, and you turned completely white!"

Alas, the same low blood pressure that made me an ideal long-distance runner also rendered me prone to passing out. I needed to be more careful.

After that event, I didn't put much effort into track. I didn't enjoy grinding lap after lap in the distance races. While some runners love the symmetry, predictability, and uniformity of the track, I much preferred the variability and unpredictability of the terrain in cross country. I delighted in not knowing what came past the crest of the next hill and seeing for miles around me. Running lap after lap with no variety was almost as boring as running on a treadmill. As a result, I seldom showed up to practice.

Toward the end of the season, another freshman Andrea and I

were slated to run the sixteen-hundred-meter at a junior varsity meet. That particular day, I froze with fear. Not only was I afraid I would collapse, but I was terrified I would fail.

As Andrea and I strolled around the track, I told her, "I don't really want to run."

It didn't help that the race was at the end of the day, and we had to worry about it all day.

"I don't, either," Andrea said.

Coach was at the varsity meet in a different location, so Coach Watkins, one of the assistant track coaches and the head football coach, was in charge.

Andrea said, "Okay, if Coach Watkins notices, we will tell him we accidentally missed the race."

"Sounds good to me," I told her.

By the time the race began, we had dodged the event. Of course, Coach Watkins found out, and he was enraged. Maybe this wasn't a good idea. I knew Coach Watkins had a temper.

"Why weren't you girls in the waiting area?" he demanded.

We both remained silent. A burly man in his forties, his reddened face steamed under his glasses.

"You didn't want to run, did you!" he stated rather than questioned.

Again, we said nothing.

"You cost our team points!" he roared.

Andrea and I walked away with our heads drooping.

"I didn't want to lie to the man," Andrea said.

"I didn't, either," I said.

Coach Watkins, much calmer, approached me later and said, "Hollie, you're a good runner. You would have placed."

"I'm sorry," I said.

What else could I say? I considered what he said and was ashamed of what I had done. I had let my fear of failure stop me from even trying. I told myself I would never let that happen again.

* * *

AS THE SPRING SEMESTER DRAGGED on, a pall of gloom settled on me again. I wondered, *Is this all there is? Barely getting up in the morning. Floating from class to class. Feeling miserable.* My classmates were nice enough, but I felt awkward, like I didn't belong. I definitely wasn't cool.

In terms of my grades, they weren't poor, but they weren't outstanding, either. I knew I was capable of so much more. It didn't help that my teachers told me I was smart and should earn all A's.

English was my best subject, and I had been enthused about taking the advanced class. Nonetheless, I didn't enjoy it like I thought I would. Switching to regular English during the spring semester, Mrs. Koss became my new English teacher. A petite woman in her forties, Mrs. Koss wore bohemian clothing and quirky eyeglasses that accented her dark-brown pixie haircut. I had already studied Greek and Roman mythology during the first semester of advanced English, which I loved, and was pleased to study it again with Mrs. Koss for the second semester of regular English. Notwithstanding, I didn't turn in my work consistently, and my grades began to slip.

In addition to teaching mythology, Mrs. Koss taught us how to investigate a topic and write a research paper. One day, she took us to the library so we could examine sources for our topic and jot notes on index cards. I, on the contrary, preferred my method and thought taking notes was pointless. Consequently, I started writing my paper.

Mrs. Koss approached me and asked, "What are you doing?"

"Writing my paper," I replied.

"You're supposed to be taking notes," she snapped. "You can't start writing your paper yet."

I seethed. I didn't see the point of it. In fact, I didn't understand the purpose for most of my academic career. It wasn't until I wrote a one-hundred-page thesis for my master's program years later that I conceded notecards were the only way to keep so many ideas from multiple sources organized.

I was so angry I didn't go to English class for three days. Instead, I went outside and wandered around campus.

When I returned to class, Mrs. Koss asked, "Where have you been?"

"I was out of town," I told her.

"Well, I am going to call your mother about your grade."

That night, as she said she would, Mrs. Koss contacted my mother. I heard Mom say, "Out of town?"

When Mom hung up, she asked, "Have you been cutting class?"

"Yeah," I said.

Mom didn't appear angry. Maybe she figured my teacher would address it the way she wanted. Mrs. Koss reported my ditching to the principal, and I had to spend three days in in-house suspension in the library. During that stretch, I simply read and did my assignments. I was relieved to be away from the other kids, where I didn't have to worry about being accepted.

After serving the suspension, I returned to class. Despite my ditching, Mrs. Koss was gracious and allowed me to complete extra-credit assignments to elevate my grade.

While we were studying mythology, Mrs. Koss asked our class to write a Choose Your Own Adventure-style story, based on one or more of the Greek myths. I thought of the time a year before when I composed the story based on the *Iliad*. That got me in major trouble. I would keep it clean this time. Since I loved Choose Your Own Adventure stories and mythology, the assignment was fun for me. I wrote a story called *The Search for Harmonia's Necklace*, which I still have.

"That was the best story I read from your class," Mrs. Koss told me later.

"Really?" I asked.

"Yes, it had the best continuity and used many elements from the myth."

I basked in the praise. Maybe I wasn't a total failure after all.

* * *

AT THE END OF THE year, the school had its awards assembly. After watching so many students win academic awards, I felt ashamed and inadequate. *I could be up there on that stage. Next year, I will try harder*, I vowed to myself.

When I arrived home that night, I stood in my backyard and gazed up at the stars. Tears rushed from my eyes, and I said, "I hate myself."

I said aloud what I had so often felt for the last year and a half.

"I am a bad person, and I keep failing. God, I promise I will turn my life around. Please help me. I will study harder next year. I will devote myself to my running. I will be a better person. Please help me," I implored.

At that moment, something inside of me changed.

CHAPTER 8

Champion

Oklahoma City

Summer – Fall 1990

MY SIX TEAMMATES AND I gathered at the starting line of our first cross country meet of the season. The sweltering August heat, filled thick with moisture, clung to our skin under our green and white uniforms.

It was my first varsity race! Adrenaline coursed through me as I jogged in place to quell my anxiety.

The official fired his gun, and we took off. Hovering near the center of the pack, I let my swifter teammates push ahead of me, clearing the field of runners. As I settled into a rhythm, I advanced on the other runners. At the mile mark, I came upon two of my teammates who had been on varsity the year before and zipped past them. *Are they okay? Why are they not running as fast as they normally do?*

Despite the enervating heat, I felt strong. One by one, I passed more runners, charging the hills and navigating the turns. With a half mile left, I broke into the front of the pack. Before I knew it, I dashed across the finish line in seventh place, finishing second fastest on the varsity team!

No one was more shocked than me. Maybe those summer runs around my house had paid off.

* * *

PART OF ME THOUGHT MY first varsity race had been a lucky break, and I wondered if I could duplicate my success. When my team and I arrived at our second meet in Little Axe, a small town in Oklahoma, I was already feeling off. I didn't feel the sense of urgency I had the week before.

When the starting gun fired, I coasted out, mesmerized by the lovely wooded area we were running through. Twigs snapped under my feet, and the scent of trees filled my nostrils.

Hollie, you're not giving it one hundred percent, I told myself.

I don't care, I retorted.

You might care later.

No, I won't.

What about your team?

Two miles later, I floated through the finish line behind some of the runners I had surpassed the week before. Head bowed, I walked up to Coach afterward and asked him, "Do you think I did well?" I needed validation that the race wasn't horrible.

He looked me in the eye and said, "You didn't do well—at all."

Coach gave it to me straight. *How could I do that?* I let myself and my team down.

* * *

I VOWED TO MYSELF I would never let that happen again. During our speed workout the next week, regret and anger surged through me.

Recurring thoughts of the race sent me blazing down the track to the brink of near exhaustion.

A cross country race was only thirteen to fourteen minutes out of my life. How hard could it be? In the moment, though, it's tricky and grueling, and if you're not careful, your brain can tell you it doesn't matter, like mine did. A runner must decide before the race she is willing to push herself to her physical limit, prepared to power through the unremitting pain, discomfort, and fatigue, despite the capricious conditions of the course, the weather, other competitors, and her own body. Unlike other sports, you can't call a timeout to rethink your game plan. Stop to walk during a two-mile race, and you might as well not finish. You can't pick up the ground you lost and still be competitive. You have to make decisions while you *and* the clock are still running.

While I mulled over possible techniques, I recalled the research paper I wrote for Mrs. Koss' class, specifically an approach I encountered in world-renowned runner Bob Glover's manual *The Competitive Runner's Handbook*. Albeit most of the content focused on the physical facets of running, one minor section resonated with me—mental preparation.

Glover described his own experiences and how lack of mental preparation sabotaged some races before he even started. Even a world-class runner experienced negative thoughts and bad races and skipped a race like I had the year before! Not only does a runner have to prime herself before the race, but she must prepare for the *thoughts* she will face brought on by the physical and mental stress during the event.

While not a novel or groundbreaking idea, to my fifteen-year-old self, it was revolutionary.

By using a technique called visualization, I could mentally

experience events before they happened. Or I could relive my best performances over and over, like playing a videotape in my brain. I could control the imagery: "see" the landmarks along the way, "hear" the crowd cheering, "smell" the air, "feel" my body gliding.

* * *

THE NIGHT BEFORE MY NEXT meet, I lay in bed and visualized the race—the warm-up area, the starting line, the course, the spectators, the competitors. I started strong. I passed other runners. I conquered hills. I repeated positive affirmations. *I will get faster this week. I am strong on hills. I run well in the heat. I move strongly and smoothly.*

I wrote my goal time on an index card and taped it to my nightstand, so it was the last thing I saw before I fell asleep and the first thing I saw when I woke up.

The following weekend, my race played out the way I imagined it. I finished within five seconds of the time I posted!

I went up to Coach and asked, "How was that?"

"Awesome!" he said. "You found redemption!"

* * *

I CONTINUED TO VISUALIZE MY future races every night before I fell asleep. Each week, I set an ambitious but realistic goal time and wrote it on my bedside index card, and each race, I ran close to my goal, setting personal records. My technique was working well!

At the same time, I realized I was fortunate that nothing drastic occurred during my races. I had to prepare for unlikely or unforeseen obstacles and incorporate them into my imagery—a shoelace comes untied, I trip and fall, a muscle cramps, the terrain turns rugged, it starts raining. I needed to visualize myself handling these potential impediments with ease and confidence. If I could conjure these images during my training runs, it would be easier to recall them at critical points.

* * *

THE TIME HAD COME FOR the West Regionals, the meet that would determine who qualified for the State meet. All the teams in the western half of the state were competing. The weather was perfect—low 70s, no wind, the sun shining bright.

As the other runners and I dashed from the starting line, I rushed near the front of the pack. Unlike the previous races, I was flying! Pain and fatigue did not consume my thoughts or my body. The race passed by in a flash. As I approached the final stretch, I was in third place. I heard Coach yell from the sideline, "Hollie, you're under thirteen!"

What? My personal record was 13:25! I had never come close to touching thirteen minutes. Upon hearing that, a spark in me ignited, and I bolted into a full sprint. I passed the second-place person and glided through the finish line at 13:00 flat, placing second! Two of my teammates and I finished 1–2–3, and our team won West Regionals!

Never had I felt such a moment of glory. I was enraptured.

A few days later, my team and I were featured in the local newspaper with a headline that said, *Top 3 Sweep Lifts Irish Girls in Regional*.

Even though I was elated, I was just as mystified by that race as I was by my mediocre performance in Little Axe. Could I experience a peak like that again at will? Could I reproduce the conditions—optimal training, rest, nutrition, mindset, and weather?

In the thirty years that have passed since then, I know the answer is no. It's not possible to replicate a moment of perfection. If I tried, I would be disappointed. I experienced a moment of "magic," a wondrous convergence that happens at best only a few times in one's life.

* * *

FOR SEVERAL DAYS, I REVELED in the glow of my victory. Coach had become like a father figure to me, and he and I fell in step on one of our runs.

"Do you think I can All-State this weekend?" I asked him.

"Oh yeah, you're definitely in the ballpark."

That Coach had confidence in me meant the world. Every night for the rest of the week, I closed my eyes and "rehearsed" the race. And, I had one advantage I didn't have before: I knew the course.

I replayed the scene ad infinitum in my mind.

On Saturday, at the State meet, crowds of spectators surrounded us, the air charged with anticipation. To think one year ago I was in the same place as one of the alternates cheering from the sideline. Now I was not only running in the State meet, but All-State was within my grasp! And my team was positioned to win the state championship!

My team and I huddled in a circle, extended our hands to the center, and yelled, "Irish!"

Lining up on the starting line, I sprinted out and back to keep myself warmed up. Both excited and nervous, this was the moment I had prepared for the last two months. I just had to finish in the top ten to achieve All-State.

Once we started, I wasn't running on air like I did the week before. Fatigue set in. My chest moved forward, my spine shortened, and my head lowered. *Focus on your form,* I told myself.

I let my shoulders and neck relax and lifted my head and spine. *There, that's it.* Even with better form, I felt myself lagging, so I swung my arms faster, impelling my legs to keep pace. As the other runners languished, the pack started thinning out. Approaching the hill after the first mile mark, every muscle in me wanted to give in. *No, do what you visualized.* I forced myself to quicken the pace and passed another runner.

With two hundred meters to go, the end was in sight! I gave it everything I had remaining and blasted through the finish line. My sudden stop in the finisher's chute left me bowed over, grabbing my knees and gasping for air.

Our assistant coach ran up to me and yelled, "Hollie Stuart, you're an All-Stater!"

I did it! I finished in sixth place!

If anyone had told me two months before that achieving All-State would be within my reach, I wouldn't have believed it, but here I was. I couldn't even say it was a dream come true because I had never imagined it.

Coach ran up to me and gave me an enormous hug.

"I knew you would do it!" he exclaimed.

"You did?" I asked him.

"You bet!" He grinned. "I saw the fire in you!"

I wasted no time cheering my teammates in. When the results were finalized, we found out our "younger, less-experienced" team had won the state championship! My teammates and I jumped up and down, clasping each other.

At that moment, I was on top of the world, and the depression and trauma of the last two years seemed miles away.

CHAPTER 9

On the Right Track

Oklahoma City
Fall 1991

IN ADDITION TO ALL-STATING FOR the state championship team, I made all A's for the semester and got inducted into the National Honor Society. I had done what I had set out to do and more with the pledge I had made in my backyard just a few months before. How could I surpass that? What if I couldn't duplicate the success I had had with cross country? What if I foundered during track like I did last year?

Despite my reservations, I decided to go for it. Otherwise, how would I know how good I could be? Just as important, I had found my tribe with the team. It was where I belonged.

Still, in some ways, track was more challenging than cross country. The meets lasted all day, and the athletes often participated in multiple events. Plus, I didn't enjoy plodding eight laps around the track, each one the same as before. I much preferred the open fields, varied terrain, rolling hills, and changing scenery of cross country courses.

For all ten of our meets that season, I competed in the thirty-two-hundred-meter and the sixteen-hundred-meter runs. Like Coach said I would, I continued to get faster, and taking home medals every week *almost* made me like track.

Everything appeared to be working in my favor by the time we made it to Regionals. I won first place in the thirty-two-hundred-meter, not only qualifying for the State meet, but getting slated to win first place at State too.

* * *

TWO DAYS BEFORE THE STATE meet, I incurred an unexpected injury—a shin splint in my left leg. Because of this, my right calf was so tight, I could hardly run at all, much less run fast. How was I supposed to race in two days?

On the day of the meet, I still couldn't run. I slumped on the couch, my hopes of winning completely dashed.

"Don't give up, honey," Mom said. "Could I take you to get your legs massaged? Would that help?"

"Well, maybe," I said.

Mom had a massage therapist come over to my house, who massaged my shin and calf for an hour. By the time she finished, I felt new again. I could run after all!

As I lined up on the starting line, the gun crackled. I took a deep breath and accelerated in the familiar counterclockwise direction. In my anxiety, I sprinted ahead, taking the front of the pack. Before I knew it, the first lap was lost in a rush of adrenaline and pounding feet. Typically, I paced myself better, but by the end of the second lap, I was gassing out, and other runners began to overtake me. Soon, I lagged a few places behind. I eased my pace and told myself it was okay. It was Little Axe all over again, but this time, I told myself I wouldn't get upset.

I crossed the finish line in third place as an official handed me the bronze medal. It was no victory, however. I had failed. I was supposed to win first and had blown the championship in the two-mile. I had let down myself and my team. I was devastated—everything I had built that season was gone.

No doubt I had made some foolish errors. All the race strategies and mental preparation I had learned throughout the year went out the window that day. I never sprinted the first lap. I never let nerves get to me like that. What made me do it that day?

Even so, those blunders overshadowed the most critical one. I had told myself two days before I was finished and wouldn't be able to run. It didn't matter that I actually could; I had told myself that I couldn't.

I learned an important lesson as an athlete that I carry with me to this day: Don't give up just because of an injury. *Find a way.*

CHAPTER 10

On Fire

Oklahoma City
1991 – 1992

I VISITED A DOCTOR AND discovered my injuries originated from a bunion on my right foot. The only long-term solution was to have corrective surgery, which incapacitated me for several weeks. When I returned to school in the late summer, I was running again, but lagging my previous times. Cross country my junior year would have to be a rehabilitation season.

While I was rehabilitating, I focused more on my studies. I had found my second tribe in school, the artsy intellectuals. As a self-professed nerd, I loved having stimulating conversations with them.

One might think that most teachers working at a Catholic high school would be Catholic. While many of them were, my greatest teachers were Unitarian Universalists. Their classes taught me to think critically and to question orthodoxy. One such class was AP English, where we studied Joseph Campbell's *Hero with a Thousand Faces.* That work had a profound influence on my worldview. One could find elements of the same story in all the world myths, which formed the basis for all the world religions. This reinforced what I had always felt was true—that all religions incorporate similar ideas and truths.

That year, we also took philosophy class for our theology credit. During the first few weeks, our teacher challenged us to study philosophers who had tried to disprove the existence of God. It disconcerted a few of my classmates, who said it made them question everything they believed. I, on the contrary, have always had an open, inquisitive mind, ever since I attended vacation Bible school and CCD classes, the Catholic equivalent of Sunday school, in Pawhuska. The studies did not faze me. It wasn't that they made me believe or not believe in the existence of God. I just thought it was fascinating to examine different possibilities. When exploring philosophical questions, curiosity was more interesting to me than certitude. And if longstanding ideas were proven wrong with new insights and discoveries, all the better. It just meant we had new potentialities to consider. Perhaps for others, pulling one string could unravel their whole belief system.

After we analyzed arguments that disproved the existence of God, our teacher reversed course and had us study philosophers who attempted to prove God's existence. Instructing us to memorize St. Thomas Aquinas' third proof for the existence of God, he often asked us, without warning, to write it out on a sheet of paper and turn it in. I don't know if that was an existential relief to my classmates, but I found it enthralling.

Overall, this class instilled in me a love of studying other religions, philosophies, and their meanings—both hidden and manifest—that I would study years later in graduate school. Catholic school, ironically, planted the seeds for my challenging religious dogma and reinforced my intellectual curiosity.

But still, I thought I had to be a good Catholic. I believed I was obligated to serve my penance for the events that occurred three years earlier.

It would take me years to allow myself to chart my own spiritual path.

Of course, exploring different forms of spirituality was in my blood. Grandma was a devout Catholic on the one hand and dabbled in various forms of spirituality on the other. Relaxing in her recliner and wearing her reading glasses, she often annotated the margins of her self-improvement and spirituality books and discussed her insights with me. She told me about visiting psychics and how she took my grandfather to see one when she was dating him in 1938! Looking back, she was also a feminist, though she might not have called herself one. Passionate about equal treatment of women in the Catholic Church, she thought women should get ordained.

"I tell the priests women should be allowed to be priests too. It's ridiculous that they aren't, but they tell me it will never happen," she said.

"Especially since so many nuns and laywomen have Masters of Divinity," I added. "They've fulfilled the same requirements to be a priest, but the Church refuses to ordain them. The *only* reason the Church won't ordain them *is* because they're women. It's a bunch of frickin' BS."

Grandma was ahead of her time, and her views resonated with mine.

We both also longed to explore the world.

"I would love to have traveled, but your grandfather didn't want to go anywhere!" Grandma said.

Grandma finally toured Europe when she was seventy years old and loved it. She told me she regretted she didn't go sooner. Therefore, when I had the opportunity to go on a school-sponsored tour of Spain in 1992, she said she would help fund it. That was the year the Summer Olympic Games were held in Barcelona, and it was a momentous time to go. Unfortunately, not enough students signed up, and the trip was canceled. My world travel—and Spain—would have to wait.

* * *

DECEMBER ARRIVED, AND IT WAS time for the Christmas dance. Custom for the girls to ask the guys, I had chosen to go stag the last couple of years. This time, I wanted to go with a date.

One afternoon, I was mingling with some of my friends at school, one of them a cute guy named Nate. The perfect combination of sports and brains, his round glasses accentuated his soft brown eyes, and his stylish clothes complemented his lean, athletic build. When I was around him, I almost got the impression he was flirting with me. No, guys did not flirt with me. However, he stroked my hair and playfully poked me in the ribs. I confessed to our mutual friend Melissa that I liked him.

She said, "He told me he likes you too."

"No, really?" I asked her.

I couldn't believe an attractive guy was interested in me.

"Do you think he'd want to go with me to the Christmas dance?" I asked.

"I can ask him if you like," Melissa said, smiling at the prospect of playing matchmaker. Unlike me, she was a shameless flirt and delighted in schooling me on boys.

"That would be awesome!" I said.

A couple of days later, Melissa reported back to me. "Yeah, he wants to go with you."

I was ecstatic! For the dance, I wore a strapless mini black velvet dress, my hair arranged in an elegant half updo. My Aunt Nancy came over again and painted my lips a glossy carnation pink and rouged my cheeks. I finished the ensemble with a pearl pendant necklace. Maybe I could be eye-catching.

* * *

AFTER THE DANCE, NATE ASKED me out on an official date! He took me to a college party in an apartment, where we lounged on the couch and watched music videos of Depeche Mode. He was quiet and shy, which made me feel comfortable with him.

Reaching for my hand, he led me to the balcony to escape the crowd. I wasn't sure if I was trembling from the frigid January air or the anticipation. I had never kissed a boy before. *What if I mess up?* We giggled nervously, as he put his lips to mine. It wasn't exactly like I imagined it, but it wasn't unpleasant, either. *This is what it is supposed to be like.* He was gentle and respectful and did not force himself on me.

Next, we heard the applause. We looked up to see several of the college students clapping and yelling, "Way to go! We give that a ten!"

Of course, my first kiss had to have spectators. We both laughed, somewhat embarrassed, as we walked back inside.

"I'm glad we gave you a good show!" I told them.

At least it broke the ice!

He was the first guy who seemed to like me and did not consider me an object to conquer.

One night, he walked me to my front porch. The cutting cold of the early evening had been replaced with a crispness in the air. We kissed in the dark, and I felt his hand move down to my chest. I froze—as if my body sensed a danger my mind had yet to grasp. Alarming thoughts invaded my mind. *The boys. The kitchen. The living room. Stop!* I thought of the last time hands had been on me.

"Uh, I can't . . ." I told him.

He backed away from me, obviously disappointed. "Okay, well, have a good night," he said, as he walked back to his car.

After that incident, our relationship fizzled out. While we remained friends, perplexing thoughts flooded my mind. *Is that what he wanted all along? To mess around, and when I told him I couldn't, he lost interest?* I was attracted to him; it just brought up too many frightening memories. Alas, the same disturbing visions and anxiety would keep returning at unexpected intervals throughout my life. Whatever the case, it seemed like a guy liking me for me was too good to be true.

* * *

SPRING ARRIVED, AND IT WAS time for track, which I both loved and hated. With intense effort, I built back up to the previous year's level, and my times got even faster. Much of that stemmed from my new racing strategy involving my split times for the thirty-two-hundred-meter.

The race has eight splits corresponding to the end of each lap. Most runners either maintain a steady pace, timing each split about the same, or they run their first four laps fast and use whatever is left in the tank for the last four laps. For the latter, the last four splits were often slower than the first four splits. Conversely, I excelled at running negative splits, in which my first four splits were slower than the last four. Running negative splits can be risky because one can get locked into a pace, and it can be challenging to speed oneself up. At the same time, it's also an optimal way to conserve energy for the last half of the race when everyone else has depleted their reserves.

By the time May arrived for the State meet, I was all jitters. It would be at the same track where I had lost the year before. Just the association frightened me. *What if I fail again?*

I knew I needed to face it—*before* the race. I had been to that track only once before, the instant I lost, and when I arrived, the memory was disquieting. In that moment, however, I was the only one there—just me and the track. I ran around the inside lane several times, fighting the memory of my loss, and tried to imagine myself prevailing. To solidify my vision, I lay on the start/finish line and visualized my victory. Unlike the year before, I was not predicted to win first. One girl from Shawnee, Oklahoma, was faster, having outrun me the couple of times I had raced her earlier that season. Another girl from Woodward I usually bested, though it was difficult to overtake her.

I still felt dubious when I left, but at least I would not be barraged by the negative images for the first time at the State meet.

On the day of the meet, I took off the whole day from school, even though my race wasn't until the afternoon. I knew I would need the rest, and it was nice to sleep in. I ate Taco Mayo for lunch, which wasn't my usual pre-race meal, but it was what sounded good.

I arrived at the meet an hour before my race, enveloped by the crowds of runners and spectators. My stomach dropped when I entered the warm-up area. *Warm up, stretch your legs, and don't go out too fast,* I told myself. *Remember, you are best when you run negative splits.*

The starting gun fired. I accelerated at a nice, steady pace, as a few runners swept ahead of me. *Pace yourself. Stick to your split times.* I was aiming for a time of 12:30, which would be a personal record for me. *Just make sure you stay on pace, and your place in the pack will take care of itself.* By the second lap, I gained on a couple of the runners.

Next, I came upon the Woodward girl. I didn't want to deal with passing her back and forth the whole race, so I did something I didn't normally do. I momentarily broke my pace and sped past her, hoping she would think I was too far ahead to catch me. It worked! I didn't have to contend with her the rest of the race.

As I picked up my pace during the second half, I felt the same way I had felt during cross country Regionals during my sophomore year. I was on fire! I seemed to float through the race, and I didn't feel the usual mounting fatigue. With three laps left, I emerged in second place. The Shawnee girl was far ahead, but I could close in on her. On the last lap, I quickened my pace, still in second place. Crossing the finish line with a time of 12:22, I beat my goal for the day and set a personal record for the thirty-two-hundred-meter!

I had overcome my fear. In an instant, that track transformed from one of my worst athletic memories to one of my best. Second place in track earned me Honorable Mention All-State. I would take it! Maybe the magic could happen more often than I initially thought. This time I did it with adequate mental preparation, an effective pacing strategy, sufficient rest, and Taco Mayo. How was I so lucky to experience it twice in two years? Even Coach affirmed a week later to the school, "Hollie ran the race of her life!"

CHAPTER 11
The Perfect Mile

Oklahoma City
1992 – 1993

IT WAS TRACK SEASON OF my senior year, the last running season of my high school career. Our team had just won the first girls' and boys' double state championship in cross country in our school history, and I had All-Stated for the third time! It was tough to top a victory like that. As a result, I didn't feel as driven as I had in the previous years, though I still performed well.

The highlight of the season was finally breaking a six-minute mile. I consistently ran the two-mile, or thirty-two-hundred-meter, race in an average of 12:30. Theoretically, I should have been able to run half that distance in under six minutes, but the fastest I had run the mile was 6:02.

Close to the end of the season, I lined up on the starting line for the sixteen-hundred-meter. Rather than pacing my laps in negative splits like I did for the thirty-two-hundred-meter, that day I decided to go all out. Maybe it was because a college recruiter was watching.

When the gun fired, I bolted ahead. Tiring quickly, I willed myself to maintain the pace. I just had to sustain it for four laps.

Accelerating into the last one hundred meters, I darted across the finish line with a time of 5:48. I not only set a new personal record—I crushed it!

That is what I needed to do. I had been running the mile wrong the whole time. I wasn't supposed to run it like the two-mile. I needed to run it for what it was—a long-ass sprint. The head coach of the university who was watching me told Coach he wanted me to run for his team. While it wasn't an NCAA Division 1 school, I was flattered to get recruited and for a coach to see me when I was "on."

The Regional meet, on the other hand, did not go well. For reasons unknown to me, I ended up nearly passing out again during the two-mile, barely crossing the finish line in third place before I collapsed—and narrowly qualifying for State.

By the time I ran in the State meet a few days later, I hadn't fully recovered. On top of that, the event was held at a different venue, one I had not run before. I took off at the start, my legs feeling like lead. As the race progressed, gravity seemed to intensify, dragging me further and further down. When I crossed the finish line, I didn't even place. Utter exhaustion had overtaken me. Unlike the State meet two years earlier, I hadn't mentally given up. My body simply didn't have it that day.

Nonetheless, I felt like a total failure. What a disappointing way to end my high school running career—not even medaling at the State meet in my best event. It was my worst performance as a varsity runner.

For the next few days, I mentally castigated myself.

"Quit being so hard on yourself. It's just a race," Mom told me.

Since she wasn't an athlete, it was hard for her to comprehend my letdown. I even ran a 10K road race, winning the women's division, but it couldn't satisfy the emptiness of my loss. I was no longer part of a team. Nothing could replace the State meet in my mind.

In spite of the loss, graduation was a happy occasion. I graduated with honors and was accepted to all the colleges I applied for. I decided to attend Rockhurst University, a small Catholic school in Kansas City, where I was going to run for the cross country and track teams. Having been awarded an academic and an athletic scholarship, I was excited to start life in a new city.

To celebrate, my friends and I ran wild all summer. When we weren't shoe polishing uproarious messages on car windows in random parking lots, we were jumping fences into people's swimming pools at night. It never occurred to us that we were eighteen and could have been arrested or—worse yet—shot. Still, it was one of the most delightful summers of my life growing up.

* * *

WHEN I ARRIVED IN KANSAS City a few months later, everything I had planned for the next four years unhinged. Because the university was in an older, and not the safest, area of the city, Mom panicked, thinking it was too dangerous. Furthermore, when I got there, it wasn't what I expected. I realized I would once again attend a small parochial school. Is that what I wanted? As someone who loved to study and immerse myself in other cultures and worldviews, I yearned for a more expansive experience.

Most of all, my mother's negative reaction had a major influence on me, and I couldn't stand to see her unhappy. Maybe I would have adjusted and enjoyed it there. Nonetheless, I decided to move back to Oklahoma and attend Oklahoma State University, where my parents had met almost thirty years earlier. I had no idea that this move would set me up to feel more lost than I had ever felt in my life.

Part Two

AGAINST THE CURRENT

CHAPTER 12

Adrift

Stillwater, Oklahoma
May 1995

A KNOCK ON THE DOOR awoke me. I fumbled in the dark to turn on my lamp, toppling a glass of water. The liquid pooled on the carpet beside my bed as my heart shuddered in my chest. For a few seconds, I felt disoriented and wondered where I was. Only the firm mattress beneath me reminded me I was in my dorm room.

Drifting in and out of consciousness, I fought to keep my eyes open and shake off the nightmares. I tried to think of something else, anything else, but the haunting visions hijacked my mind.

Mom was lying in a hospital bed, about to pass on. Holding my hand, she gazed up at me.

"Now I want you to live a happy life and don't *feel sad for me," she said.*

"But, Mom, I am not ready for you to go," I cried.

My dad, who had been alive this whole time, also appeared. I was enraged.

"Where have you been the last twelve years?" I asked him. "Why didn't you tell me you are alive?"

Rousing me from my dream, I heard my mother's voice outside the door. A surge of emotions rushed through me. *She's alive! Thank God!* Opening the door, Mom found me sprawled in bed, my room in disarray.

"Honey, what's wrong?" she asked.

Dark bags hung under my eyes, my face red from hours of weeping. My body was shaking. Except for dozing off a few minutes before, I'd been awake for almost three days.

"Honey, what is it?" she asked, peering into my sunken eyes.

How can I tell her? How can I tell anyone what I have gone through the past few days? I wrestled overwhelming nausea, the surrounding air closing around my throat. *When was the last time I ate, drank, or slept? Three days maybe.* It was the end of my sophomore year, and I couldn't even take my final exams.

My mother sat on my bed, and I collapsed into her arms.

"Honey, tell me what happened," she said. "You look like you're having a nervous breakdown."

"I can't talk about it," I said through sobs.

Nervous breakdown? Is that what I'm having? How did I even get to this point?

"Here, let's get you packed up and go home," Mom said.

* * *

BACK IN OKLAHOMA CITY, I woke up just enough to flip beneath the covers and noticed I was perspiring. I threw the covers off and rolled to the cool, untouched portion of sheets on the other side of my bed.

My days and nights were plagued by terrifying dreams . . . *I was drowning, unable to breathe.*

I squeezed my fingers and shook them, as if I could fling the night terror from me. The lids of my eyes grew heavy, but I didn't dare fall back asleep.

Mom was so worried about me. She had never seen me like this before, and I couldn't find the words to tell her what was happening. I felt like the light in my soul had been extinguished, and I wondered if I would ever feel happy again.

After a week at home, the rising swells of panic finally ceased—only for a horrifying depression to take its place. *How did I get here, and how did everything go so terribly wrong?*

* * *

AT FIRST, I LOVED OSU. I couldn't help feeling excited, ready for my life to soar. By sheer luck, I moved into Bennett Hall, the most diverse residence hall on campus. Never mind it was the last hall anyone chose because of its lack of air-conditioning. Bennett was one of those antiquated buildings that seemed to hold the scents and essences of everyone who had lived there over the years. Like an old cloth easy chair, it was musty but comfortable—except in the baking heat of late August when we roasted in the confines of its walls. Best yet, it was where my dad lived when my parents started dating in the early '60s.

As with many structures that have been someone's home, it retained a familial coziness amid the current institutional milieu. One side housed the athletes, while the other side accommodated everyone else. Encountering international students, racial and religious minorities, and members of the LGBTQ community, I spent hours in the lobby becoming acquainted with them. I found their perspectives refreshing and fascinating. This wasn't like Catholic schools, where most students were Catholic, affluent, and white.

Most of all, it was liberating for no one to have known me before. I could bust out and be myself—HoHo! Unlike the rigid constraints of Catholic school, college life was unbounded, an utter culture shock for me. Consequently, I cut loose, lapsing to my natural inclinations—staying up all night with friends, going to parties, and sleeping through my early-morning classes. I became fast friends with my roommate and the other girls in the hall. We soon fell into a pattern of gathering in the hallway at night, eating pizza, and pulling pranks on each other.

I wasn't worried about my studies, though. Having tested out of twenty-one hours of general education classes, I rushed ahead. In addition, choosing journalism and broadcasting as my primary field of study, I made satisfactory grades and found the curriculum straightforward.

At the same time, boys were a major distraction. Good-looking men wandered campus in abundance, and I had a crush on about ten of them. To my surprise, a couple of them even asked me out—men I considered out of my league. My inexperience and awkwardness with dating, however, ensured it didn't go anywhere.

Although I didn't realize it at the time, I felt particularly drawn to either churchgoers or presumably gay men. Based on my previous experiences, I suppose they were the only ones who seemed unthreatening to me. For the former, I sensed a certain level of respect and safety, and for the latter, their gentleness and kindness. Other men I saw as potential predators. I learned when I was a child with Jason that I couldn't trust most boys, and I generally avoided them. Moreover, I was attuned to boys and could tell the difference between the male gaze that conveyed interest and attraction and the one that pushed, insisted, and claimed. Often a fine line separated assertiveness from aggression, and I evaded aggressive overtures at all costs.

The second semester, I fell in love with James, a guy I met at the local Catholic church. He was my age and cute, though not classically handsome. With shaggy brown hair and eyes that narrowed into slits when he smiled, he was quiet and shy. Despite that, his social awkwardness endeared me to him, and I felt comfortable around him. We didn't have much in common, other than he originally came from a small town like me, and we both loved astronomy. Our conversations were awkward and stilted with one or both of us usually blushing.

Toward the end of the semester, it seemed like he might be interested in me when he asked me to go cycling with him around the lake. We spent the afternoon riding and talking, and I felt a sense of safety I hadn't felt with any guy in a while. When we returned to my dorm, we stood under a tree in front of the edifice.

James took both of my hands in his. He gazed at me and said, "Have a good summer, Hollie," and moved closer. *Is he really going to kiss me?*

"Whewwwww!" I heard. I turned to see my friends hanging out the window whooping at us. *Damn them! Why were there always people watching when I kissed a guy?*

"Hey, get out of here!" I yelled.

I laughed; I would have done the same thing had the roles been reversed. Flustered, I turned back to James. Instead of kissing him, I hugged him and said, "I hope to see you this summer when I come to town."

In the moment, I lost my nerve, and it was gone. It didn't matter, though. I was in love!

When I left for Oklahoma City the next day, I kicked myself for not kissing him. *How did I mess that up? Maybe we will have another chance during the summer.*

***

THE ENTIRE SUMMER BREAK, I imagined our first kiss and what it would be like. I couldn't wait for school to start, so we could resume our near romance.

I didn't know I would never have another chance with him.

When I returned to school, James didn't meet me with the same excitement. Instead, he withdrew and avoided me. *What happened to change his feelings?* The entire fall semester of my sophomore year, I brooded over how I could win him over. I anguished over what I could have done differently, and why he didn't love me.

For most of the fall semester, I hardened myself against the rejection. Then November came—the month I had dreaded every year since I was thirteen—and the dam broke. The onslaught of emotions I hadn't allowed myself to feel consumed me, and my heart shattered. My grades nosedived, and I wondered how I would make it through the semester.

***

BY GOOD FORTUNE, I BUMPED into my friend Ron at church.

"Hey, do you want to go with me to meet Tom for coffee?"

"Sure!" I said.

Tom was another friend from church I'd had a crush on since the first week of freshman year. Six years older than me, Tom was in the Army and had traveled all over the world. I found him and his overseas stories exhilarating.

"Hollie! How is my running friend?" asked Tom. "How are things going with James?"

"Nothing's going on now," I said, trying not to sound too despondent.

"That's too bad. I tried to get him to go out with you."

In most ways, Tom was the opposite of James—gregarious, charismatic, and worldly. Striking with a muscular build, triumphal posture, close-cropped sandy blond hair, and iridescent green eyes, I could stare at his face all day.

A couple of days after Ron and I met Tom for coffee, Tom called me to go with him to dinner and a movie! He took me to a Victorian home that had been converted into a cozy Italian restaurant and to see the new *Star Trek: Generations* movie. With Tom, I was charmed and dazed in equal degree. It seemed like he had lived twice as much as me and had seen more of the world than anyone I knew. I couldn't help but be drawn to his endless chatter, seeming self-assurance, and audaciousness. Tom could and did talk to *anyone*. Once he started yammering, he kept going, like a car with bad brakes, unable to slow down, much less stop, unless by an outside force.

After that night, we saw each other almost every day. Meeting after class, we usually ran or walked around campus. Often, he invited me over to the one-room shack he lived in and cooked me dinner. While we were not sexually involved, he often held me in his arms when we were watching a movie, bringing me the comfort I needed and craved. I didn't know if we were dating or good friends, but his company lifted my spirits. When I was with Tom, I forgot about James and could laugh and carry on with him for hours.

Right before Christmas, Tom asked me if I would join him to

see *The Nutcracker* in Tulsa. Now I no longer needed to question our relationship; this was a date! Since it was a fancy engagement, my mother sent me an elegant black dress, and I had my hair and makeup done. Although I had been around him almost every day for the last two months, I was nervous. I thought I would somehow blunder.

When Tom picked me up, he was wearing shorts and a flannel shirt over his T-shirt.

"Is that what you're wearing?" I asked.

He hadn't yet changed into his suit. Since we were short on time, he had me drive his massive '70s two-door Ford with a V-8 engine, while he dressed in the back seat. Anytime I hit the brakes, he flew forward.

"Hey, easy on the brakes!" he yelled.

"I've never driven one of these boats before. This thing is as old as I am! And I'm in high heels!"

Then it became a game.

"You're doing good, Holls," he said.

"Oh, yeah?" I asked. I made a sharp turn as he put on his tie—just enough to fling him to the side.

"This is fun!" I said, laughing.

"What are you trying to do to me?" he asked.

My erratic driving caught the attention of one of the OSU police. After I pulled over, the cop peered in my window to see me dressed up—and Tom in the back seat in his underwear.

"What's going on here?" the cop asked.

"Oh, I'm just driving while he changes. We're trying to make it to see *The Nutcracker* in Tulsa."

"Can this car drive?" the cop asked.

"Yes, it's fine," Tom said. "She's just not used to it."

"Well, it's older than I am," I said.

"Just be careful," the cop said.

"That was awesome!" I said as the cop drove off.

"Okay, I'm taking back the wheel."

* * *

THROUGHOUT THE EVENING, I FELT excitement laced with anxiety. I didn't have much dating experience and didn't know what to do with someone six years older. *Are we supposed to hold hands while we watch the performance?* After years of fearing a guy would make a move on me, I, for once, wanted Tom to take the lead. Unlike the times we had spent together before, Tom was unusually quiet and pensive. *Am I a boring date?*

After we arrived back in Stillwater, he asked, "Do you want to go to Minnesota for Christmas break with me?"

I guess he still wanted to spend time with me.

"I'd really like to," I told him, "but my mother is sick with the mumps, and I want to go home to see her."

"Okay, I'll see you when I get back. Have a Merry Christmas," he said.

I lingered for a moment to see if he would try to kiss me. After he made no move, I exited the car both confused and relieved.

CHAPTER 13

Abyss

Stillwater

Winter – Spring 1995

EVERY DECEMBER FOR THE LAST seven years had dampened both the surroundings and my spirit with its fleeting days and overcast skies. This year, however, I felt hopeful. It was so subtle and gradual that by the time I realized what was happening, it was too late to shield myself. I was besotted with yet another guy. I knew it wasn't good for me—this sudden neediness that had come over me, this deep yearning to be with Tom. Still, I couldn't wait to see him again.

When I returned to Stillwater in January, I called him, excited to hear his voice for the first time in weeks. *An out-of-service message?* I furrowed my brow and glanced down at the keypad. I must have misdialed. I punched his number again and received the same message. *What's going on?*

Puzzled, I went to the church to see if anyone knew his whereabouts.

"Have you heard from Tom?" I asked Ron.

"Oh, yeah. He moved to Tulsa a few days ago," he said.

"What?" I was stunned.

He didn't even call to tell me. And I had no way to reach him.

With that realization, winter arrived fierce and unrelenting with its cold days, chilly rains, and fading landscapes. Two guys gone in the last few months. *Why does this keep happening to me?*

The depression and heartbreak of the last two months returned in full force. I could hardly focus on my studies, and my grades began to lapse. Worst of all, the mumps was taking a toll on my mother, and her condition was worsening. Without a car, I couldn't go back to Oklahoma City to see her. *What if she dies? Vanishes just like my father?*

I was spiraling and needed someone to clutch me from the vortex, so I began to see a therapist for the first time in my life. While she helped me cope with my shock and grief, what could I do about my mother?

"Mom, I should come home," I told her on the phone.

"No, I will be fine, honey. Just concentrate on your school."

I didn't know if she was minimizing her illness, or if I was overreacting. I started having dreams that she passed—my worst nightmare. Moreover, my grandfather's health had been deteriorating for some time, and his outlook didn't look favorable. I felt powerless, knowing I could do nothing.

Toward the end of the semester, my therapist announced that the next week would be our last session. I was shocked. Why hadn't she warned me, so I could prepare?

The following week, the unthinkable happened—the Oklahoma City bombing. How could something so ghastly happen in my town?

While I didn't personally know anyone who was killed in the bombing, I had friends who lost loved ones. Plus, the emotional proximity was overwhelming. I had worked down the street from the

Murrah building, the one decimated, just the previous summer.

It was all too much. The people I relied on most were either disappearing from my life or on the brink of dying. My city was bombed. I felt pressure building in my chest as if I were sinking underwater. The thin rope mooring me snapped, and I was swept into a turbulent sea.

Until then, I had endured all the pain with stoical silence. Now I felt a seething resentment and anger for all that had been left unsaid, and I couldn't say, for all that was broken and couldn't be mended. In an explosion of rage, I threw my phone at the window, shattering a pane of glass.

Adrift and vanquished, I finally broke.

CHAPTER 14
Staying Afloat

Stillwater
1996 – 1997

MOM BEGGED ME NOT TO return to school. "Just take a year off," she said. *And do what? Stay at home and do nothing?* School and running were all I knew.

To my relief, my mother recovered from the mumps. It *was* worse than she let on, as she later referred to it as the time she almost died. It was good to spend the summer with her to recover. Working as a summer intern at a local nonprofit, I assisted victims of the bombing. Given my state of mind, that job was not ideal for my mental health and became one of the reasons I wanted to leave Oklahoma City. The specter of the bombing still loomed over the entire metro. Moreover, what right did I have to feel depressed when I saw people firsthand who had lost loved ones in the bombing, or had somehow survived the bombing? At least I wasn't going through that.

On the other hand, the thought of returning to Stillwater terrified me. After reading as many self-improvement books as I could over the summer, I returned for the fall semester determined not to fall apart.

During my first week, I visited the church to see if I would bump into any of my friends.

"We have a new campus minister," one of them said, "and she's a nun! Her name is Sister Sheila."

"Cool!" I said. "I am going to check out this nun."

I had just finished running and was wearing my athletic shorts and a tank top, my damp ponytail clinging to my neck. The priests didn't like me showing up to church like that, but I was an athlete. I pointed out they wouldn't have an issue with one of the college guys donning gym shorts and a T-shirt.

I walked into the office and beheld a woman in her sixties with short, curly brown hair and glasses, wearing simple pants and a button-up shirt. She didn't wear a habit like many nuns.

"Hi, Sheila," I greeted her, as I plopped down in one of her chairs. "I'm Hollie."

"Well, hello, Hollie," she said. "I take it you're one of the students."

"Yes," I said. "It's nice to meet you. Where have you come from?"

"I was the campus minister at UC – Boulder in Colorado," she said.

The Berkeley of Colorado. My hippy-dippy sensibilities perked up, and I felt an immediate kinship with her.

"Coming from Boulder to Stillwater has been a shock," she told me. "I can't believe how conservative it is here."

"I know what you mean," I said. "And I haven't even lived outside Oklahoma. My dad graduated from UC – Boulder."

"Really? Tell me more about him."

Sheila had lost her mother when she was a child, like I had lost my father, so we understood each other in a way most people didn't.

Moreover, she got my humor. Having been submerged in so much darkness the last few months, I felt my light return when I was around Sheila. She not only saw my light in one of my darkest moments, but brought it out in me, along with my silliness and my confidence. She helped me remember who I was.

Maybe my light hadn't been extinguished after all.

My church friends were shocked at what I would say in front of her. I swore and told inappropriate jokes, to which Sheila would smile and stifle a giggle, if not laugh out loud.

"She's a nun," my friends said.

"She's a person like everyone else," I replied.

Unlike my friends, I didn't put priests and nuns on a pedestal.

Sheila later told me I was the only student who spoke to her like she was a normal person. She not only accepted my "irreverence," she loved it. More than that, with Sheila, I felt safe to be my total self, a gift I would experience with only a few people throughout my life.

I knew at one point I would have to introduce Sheila to Grandma, since they were from the same generation. The next time Mom and Grandma came to town, I asked Sister Sheila to join us for dinner.

At Stillwater Bay, one of the more upscale restaurants in town, Grandma, seated next to Sheila, nudged her with her elbow and asked, "So, do you have a girlfriend?"

Sister Sheila laughed and said, "No, do you?"

I slapped my palm to my face and remembered Grandma saying something to me years before about most nuns being lesbians, which wasn't true. Luckily, Sheila had a great sense of humor and didn't take offense. At last, someone who could dish it back to Grandma!

* * *

DESPITE SOME ENCOURAGING IMPROVEMENTS OVER the previous year, my moods still vacillated. Some mornings, I woke up bursting with energy and ambition, as if I could accomplish anything. Other mornings, however, I retreated inward. On such days, I became withdrawn, trapped inside my head, plagued by the awful memories of the prior year. I would crawl back into bed and curl into myself.

For classes, I enrolled in a full course load my junior year, opting not to finish the courses from the prior semester. Too much pain resided there, and I hadn't enjoyed the journalism classes. I didn't get to write about topics that energized me. That year, I took a history of economic thought class that I loved, which inspired me to change my major to economics with minors in history and Spanish. I figured economics and history were a suitable compromise, engaging my interest in social sciences.

In addition, I made running a priority. It had been my lifeline time and again. After I had run for a while, my heart galloping to the point of exhaustion, I felt as though I had entered another realm. I could focus on the movement of my body and the rasping of my lungs as I ran unrestrained through the streets of Stillwater. Such iron self-discipline invigorated me physically and emotionally. Aside from socializing with my friends, running was the only time I could quiet my anxiety and dispel my fears.

Yet even running could become lonely if not enjoyed with other people. I soon started training with the Stillwater High School cross country team and the Stillwater Running Club. Other than competing on the collegiate team, I noticed there wasn't a niche for recreational college runners. I spoke to the leaders of the Stillwater Running Club and asked if they would support the formation of an OSU Running Club. They agreed and even let me use similar language from their charter. Becoming the first president of the club, I hoped to build a solid membership of runners and join like-minded athletes.

Also, I started seeing a new therapist, hoping I could work through all the trauma I had experienced. With the influence of a close friend, I got my grades back on track. For the first time in college, I even made the dean's list! Nonetheless, I was still plagued with nightmares, bouts of depression, and anxiety. *Why do I have to work so hard just to feel okay?* I thought. Some days, I felt like I was paddling and going nowhere.

* * *

SENIOR YEAR, THE TORRENT STRUCK me again. When I was working at the front desk of my residence hall, a middle-aged man who worked for the maintenance crew showed up and made continuous advances toward me. Intrusive thoughts of the incidents from grade school came to mind, and I froze in terror. I started calling out for my shifts, doing everything I could to avoid him. Concerned about my sudden callouts, my friends and the university intervened, forbidding the man from approaching me again. But a forgotten fear had already unlocked inside of me and permeated my whole being. I had been doing so well—only to come undone.

Shortly after the situation was resolved, my mother and sister came to town. I was still rattled, and Mom couldn't understand why. Of course, she didn't know the situation echoed untold events from years ago. Still, I was frustrated with her for not understanding.

To quell my anxiety, I ran around campus in the afternoons. A woman pulled over and said, "Hey, I've noticed you booking it out here every day. Have you ever thought about running for the cross country team? I'm the coach."

I hadn't, but perhaps this was what I needed.

Honored she had stopped to speak with me, I told her, "No, but I might think about it."

"Here is my number," she said, handing me a card. "Call me later, and we'll talk about it."

The coach didn't seem concerned I hadn't run competitively in three years. Somehow, I allowed her flattery to get the best of me and talk me into walking onto an NCAA Division 1 team. It included running twice per day and waking up at six a.m., something I hadn't done in years. If I thought the training in high school was rigorous, it was nothing compared to college level. *Why run fifty to seventy miles per week to train for 5K races?* That seemed like overkill. Ultimately, the training proved to be too much. I soon transformed into a zombie and had no energy for anything else—my classes or my job. Worst of all, it completely sucked the joy out of running for me—so much that I seldom ran for the next thirteen years. Of course, quitting the team only exacerbated my sense of failure. Lapsing into a major depression, my grades slumped again. I was back where I was two years before.

While my running and academic achievements had been crucial for restoring my self-confidence in high school, they taught me an equally adverse mentality. Unconsciously, I learned to base my self-worth on my performance. With no collegiate academic or athletic accomplishments to claim, I felt useless.

What would I do now that I was about to graduate? Going to graduate school didn't feel right. If I wasn't managing my studies well, how would I expect to do so in graduate school? Maybe I could join the Peace Corps. That would allow me to see the world and do humanitarian work. Mom, however, thwarted that plan. She said,

"That's not why you went to college. You went so you could get a good job." *Whatever that was.* I see now my mother most likely feared me leaving the country for two years. Departing Stillwater with a diploma and a mediocre transcript in hand, I had no idea what I wanted to do or what I would do next.

Part Three

LIGHT ON THE HORIZON

CHAPTER 15
Finding My Stride

Oklahoma City
1997 – 2003

BACK IN OKLAHOMA CITY, I felt like a castaway on uncertain seas. I envied my friends who had started their careers and even had jobs lined up right after graduation. I, on the other hand, was five months out from graduation with no job or prospects. I couldn't even glimpse a vision for my future beyond the next week.

While I knew I wasn't prepared to go to graduate school, I didn't see myself working in a corporate environment, either. Nonetheless, I saw no other option than to join the business world, a place I had never envisioned myself, nor for which I deemed myself suitable.

"I don't know if there is a place in the world for me," I cried to my mother.

"Oh, honey, of course there is," she said. "God will find the perfect place for you."

I wasn't so sure about that.

After enduring the anguish of the last few years, I relished the soothing presence of my mother and grandmother. Grandma, who was committed to helping me build my confidence, gave me some practical motivational tapes to listen to. We both loved self-improvement programs and often shared what we learned with each other.

The books and tapes helped somewhat, but the only way I would build self-assurance was by facing my fears. I was in that awkward position of not having enough experience to get a professional job, while my college degree overqualified me for other positions. It didn't help that I kept interviewing and not getting hired.

One day, my fortune changed when I interviewed for a management position, one I considered out of reach. I had never imagined myself in management and knew I didn't have the requisite experience, but I also didn't have anything to lose. Arriving at the interview in my classic navy business suit, I looked the part, even if I didn't believe I fit it.

Ken, the director and a man in his fifties, stood up from behind his desk and extended his hand to shake mine. Although he towered over me, his smile and easygoing manner put me at ease. After we sat down, he pushed up his glasses and studied my resume. A successful business executive, Ken was also an intellectual and had a passion for learning like I did. During our conversation, he didn't ask me one question about the job I applied for. He, instead, asked me about my academic and athletic accomplishments, what books I enjoyed, and what I thought made an effective manager. He later told me what impressed him most about me was the books I had read and how thoughtful my answers to his questions were. Leaving the interview feeling optimistic, I was ecstatic the next day when he offered me the position!

This kind man, who had three decades of management and sales experience, was willing to train a young woman like me, who had no expertise in either field. I later asked him why he had hired me.

He said, "I liked you, and I could tell you were smart and willing to learn."

During my first few months in the role, Ken mentored me, providing me with a solid introduction to management. Just as my confidence started to improve, however, he announced he was to leave the company. At first, I was distressed, not knowing how I would continue growing without his expert guidance.

Sure enough, the workplace culture changed after his departure. For this reason, I resigned a few months later to assume a management position with another company. As I became more experienced, I also became more self-assured. Even so, I still felt inadequate, that somehow, I had fooled everyone. And no external evidence seemed to convince me otherwise. In my first three years of management, I got promoted three times, thinking, *They don't really know me. I'm not as good as they think I am.* I maintained this false belief even when I was elevated to middle management in my thirties, overseeing an operation of two hundred people.

I had never envisioned myself in corporate management, but here I was. On the contrary, I had pictured myself working in an academic setting or living abroad. Professors had even advised me to remain in school, that I would enter the "real world" soon enough. To my surprise, I enjoyed the "real world" much more than working as a full-time student. It gave me a sense of self-sufficiency I didn't possess before.

What was next? Meet a nice man, get married, and have kids? Isn't that what every woman wants? I thought so without seriously thinking about it.

I dated frequently in my twenties, usually seeing someone only once or twice. Either I wasn't interested in the guy, or he wasn't interested in me. A couple of men even wanted to marry me, but I knew I wasn't ready.

Grandma, of course, wanted me to find a quality husband.

"Don't pray for a specific person," she said. "Pray for the *right* person."

In reality, I wasn't sure I ever wanted to get married. Part of me thought it seemed suffocating, and I was afraid it would force me to abandon my dreams. More than anything, I longed to travel the world and study other cultures. On the one hand, the idea of having a boyfriend sounded romantic; on the other hand, so did the thought of living as a solo woman adventurer/traveler, who didn't need a man.

* * *

I AM GRATEFUL FOR THOSE years I got to spend with Grandma. When her health declined, and she had to move into a nursing home, I still visited her.

"Grandma, remember when you said you were taking me to New Mexico because I would start ignoring you?"

"Yes," she said. "You never did."

"I told you I wouldn't!"

On the last full day of her life, she lay in bed sleeping, the morphine keeping her comfortable.

"I love you so much, Grandma," I said, tears trickling down my face, as I held her hand. "We had the best time together."

Grandma's eyes bolted open, and she sat up. In a flash of clarity, she contemplated my face, and I knew she had heard me. Closing her eyelids, she inched back down in the bed. I knew it would be the last time I saw her. Sure enough, she passed away the following morning in her sleep.

Grandma had been my inspiration and my bulwark. Now she would be my spirit guide. "Grandma, I am going to travel the world one day," I told her, "and I know you'll be with me."

CHAPTER 16

The Sweetest Thing

Oklahoma City
2005 – 2006

As I STRODE BETWEEN THE business towers downtown, a gorgeous young man with espresso hair approached me. *That's him,* I thought. Donning a sharp suit, he was even more handsome in person than in his photo.

His questioning eyes studied me and widened in recognition as he drew closer.

"Hi, I'm Jay," he said through a bashful grin.

Without thinking, I embraced him. "It's great to meet you in person. I'm Hollie."

We had spoken on the phone the last few weeks, and I found his warm voice soothing.

Even so, Jay was never more than the object of an exciting, wishful desire. To explore possibilities with him transcended anything I imagined. As we sat across from each other at the restaurant, I discerned a softness and a serenity I had never sensed in a guy before. I loved how he followed his comments with a question and searched my eyes like he really wanted to know me. I was smitten.

After we had been chatting for about three months, I asked Jay to go hiking with me in the Wichitas. For someone who was not an experienced hiker and climber, Jay glided over the valley of boulders, bounding from one rock to another. In between the massive stones, small groves of post oak and juniper in their springtime glory scratched our legs. On one of the grander boulders, Jay reached down to help me. Of course, I could have climbed it myself, but I wasn't going to turn down an opportunity to hold his hand.

As soon as we reached level ground, we both stood and regarded each other for a couple of seconds. For a moment, I thought he wanted to kiss me. *No, I must be imagining things. Guys this good-looking aren't interested in me.*

"Let's head down *this* trail," I blurted, continuing along the path toward the high granite bluffs. As we emerged from the canyon, we beheld a sweeping vista of the tall cliffs, massive granite boulders, and broad, lush valley that wound between the towering Twin Rocks and mountains in the lower part of the canyon. A small creek meandered through the valley, flowing out into the farmland at the foot of the mountains.

Out of breath, I said, "Wow, this is beautiful! Let's stop here and take this in."

Lying on the stone precipice, we gazed at the late afternoon sky and occasionally glanced at each other. Instinctively, I grasped his hand. I'm not sure where the boldness came from. In any case, he didn't pull away.

Jay turned his head to face me, his blue eyes gleaming in the sunlight. Pressing up on his elbow, he leaned over and covered my lips with his. It was gentle, electrifying, and transcendental. I had never experienced a kiss like that before. Time and place didn't matter, nor did the unyielding rock surface we lay on.

Several minutes later, chattering hikers broke our reverie. I glimpsed the burnt-orange sun receding beneath the horizon and said, "We'd better start heading back, so we don't have to hike in the dark."

We both rose, and Jay gripped my hand. As we trekked back, our fingers interlaced, he paused every few minutes and said, "I want to make sure you still like me," and gave me another gentle, lingering kiss.

This must be a dream.

As we drove home, he asked, "Would you like to come to my apartment and watch a movie?"

"Sure," I said.

Wadded clothes, empty takeout containers, and dishes cluttered his apartment—the quintessential bachelor pad. As soon as we entered, we made for the couch and resumed what we had started on the boulder a few hours earlier.

Jay broke away from me and said, "I have something to tell you. I have only been with one person, and I don't have any protection."

Wait, does he just assume I'm going to sleep with him? The moment of vulnerability made him even more endearing.

"Oh, that's okay," I said. "I haven't been with anybody."

"What?" Jay was shocked.

"Uh, yeah," I said.

I always felt ridiculous admitting that to a guy at my age. Sensing my unease, he touched my hand and said, "It's all right."

This revelation usually startled men, and they backed off, not wanting to alarm me.

Instead, Jay kissed me and took the lead with a gentle insistence I had never experienced before.

"Wanna fool around in there?" he asked, nodding toward his

bedroom. "It might be more comfortable."

Normally that proposition would frighten me, but I trusted him.

Several minutes later, I could see where it was going—and I couldn't go through with it. "Jay, I'm not ready for this."

"You don't have to do *anything* you're uncomfortable with." He pulled me into his arms, and we fell asleep.

* * *

I AWOKE THE NEXT MORNING in a sleepy haze, the soft light spilling through the window. I peered over at Jay, sleeping peacefully.

He's so beautiful. Not just physically. I thought his essence was beautiful. I sensed a sweetness and innocence in him that I hadn't experienced with other guys I dated. Even though I hardly knew him, I felt an immediate comfort with him I had never felt before.

I leaned over and kissed him.

He woke up and smiled. "Good morning. What did I do?" he asked.

"Nothing," I said, beaming back at him.

He drew me down and kissed me, all my fears and insecurities melting away.

"Are you *sure* you aren't ready?" he asked, chuckling at my unexpected moxie. "Do you want to . . . ?"

In almost every other conceivable situation, I couldn't imagine saying yes. However, this was a moment of perfection.

"Yes," I said without hesitation.

For the first time, I felt no reluctance, no dread, only a nervous thrill.

He was so kind and gentle with me. For one blissful moment,

all my fears and doubts abandoned me, floating away like wisps of haze. I forgot about the damage the boys had done to me. A broken part of me had been made whole.

Jay folded his arms around me and pulled me into his circle of warmth.

"How are you?" he asked.

"Wonderful," I said, smiling.

In the drowsy aftermath of passion, I glimpsed him drifting back to sleep.

"Jay, I don't want to see anyone else."

His eyes fluttering, he said, "I don't want to see anyone else, either."

We lay in each other's arms for a few more hours. While I wanted nothing more than to lie there all day, I had to go to work.

Jay groaned and tightened his hold around me. "Don't leave."

"I wish I didn't have to," I said, "but the employees will wonder where I am."

"Okay, call me later," he said through his shy grin.

* * *

THE NEXT DAY, THE FULL reality of what happened hit me. So much had occurred in the last twenty-four hours. I'd had one of the greatest experiences of my life, and it both exhilarated and frightened me.

Our experience weighed on Jay too.

"I feel guilty," he told me. "I think about my ex-girlfriend. She was supposed to be the One," he said.

It unnerved him that he had been intimate with anyone else.

"I didn't mean to take anything from you," he said.

"No, it was perfect. You didn't take anything from me. But

maybe we should slow down for a while," I said.

"Yeah, I think so, too," he said.

* * *

A FEW DAYS LATER, I invited Jay to go to Tulsa with me to visit some friends. Seeing him again elated me, and I almost kissed him. During the drive, a silence settled over us, and we exchanged smiles in between stolen glances. We had gotten close physically, but still knew so little about each other. When we strolled around a lake later in the day, he grazed my back, and a current of electricity ran through me.

Once we returned home, I called my friend Miggi in anguish.

"Oh my god, I am a ho," I lamented.

"No, you're not a ho," she reassured me.

Even I knew that "watching a movie" didn't really mean watching a movie.

"Seriously, Holls, it's about time. Your nun license expired a long time ago."

"Yeah, the nunnery is out for me." I laughed, thinking how I would tell Sister Sheila.

"You've never done anything like this in your life," Miggi said. "Cut the crap they taught us in Catholic school. Don't overthink it. Just ride the wave and enjoy it."

Miggi was one to follow her feelings and not overthink everything like I did.

"It was so hard for me not to touch him, and it's been ten days," I said.

"Just go for it," she said.

"All right, I think I will. Love you!"

"Love you more! Bye, Ho!"

* * *

A FEW DAYS LATER, JAY came over to my place. This time, neither of us hesitated; we collapsed into each other's arms, our kiss turning from tender to eager to passionate.

"Are you okay with this?" I asked.

"Yeah, I just needed some time," he said.

"I did, too," I told him.

Jay swooped me up and carried me off. Maybe this was an experience we both needed. As adults who never had the carefree high school or college romance most people had—mine due to trauma and his due to his stringent religious upbringing—we both longed for it.

He was the first man I felt truly safe with. Since he didn't have much more experience, I didn't feel intimidated. Likewise, he told me his former girlfriend had been more practiced, which daunted him, but he didn't feel that way with me. At last, we both found someone on the same level and felt a comfort we hadn't felt with anyone else. Making up for lost time, we launched into an intense affair.

We became the absurd "teenage" couple who couldn't keep their hands off each other. When we went out, he held my hand or put his arm around me. "I want everyone to know you're mine," he said.

I couldn't believe a guy so handsome would go for me.

* * *

ABOUT A MONTH LATER, JAY held me down and started tickling me.

"You look so cute when I tickle you," he said.

I couldn't help but laugh. "Stop!" I screamed.

Jay thought it was a game, but fear gripped me. It started out faint, like something lurking at the bottom of a deep lake, only to rush to the surface.

"Please stop," I begged him.

Jay stopped his tickling and peered into my eyes. "Are you okay?"

"Don't ever pin me down," I cried.

He looked concerned, his gaze questioning.

"These guys forced themselves on me when I was thirteen," I told him.

It took Jay a few seconds to absorb what I said. His jaw tightened, and he said, "If I ever saw those guys, I'd let them have it."

I had never seen Jay angry. His eyes met mine with his characteristic gentleness, and he said, "I want you to know I will *never* do that to you."

I sighed with relief, still crying.

"Come here," he said. "Let's just lie here."

I fell asleep in his arms and knew he was telling the truth.

* * *

WHILE PARTS OF OUR ROMANCE seemed magical, glaring disparities emerged. He was content to go days without speaking to me, which unearthed all my insecurities. *Maybe he's using me. Maybe there's another girl. He's going to leave me and disappear. He's too good to be true, anyway.* One time, I put him to the test and didn't call him to see how long it would take him to contact me. He waited an entire week. Assuming we would get together, he asked me about coming over, and I told him I already had plans. He seemed surprised and made plans to see me the following weekend.

When I saw him outside my apartment, he lifted me, twirled me, and kissed me. "I have missed you!"

"Have you really?"

I was so happy to see him, but I held back.

"What's wrong?" he asked.

I cried. "You're just using me. You only call me when you want to come over."

"No, no, no," he said, embracing me. "I just need time to myself sometimes."

Thinking of Tom from college, I said, "I am afraid you're going to leave me. Is there another girl?"

"No, there's no one else," he assured me. "I'm sorry. I'll do better."

True to his word, he called me more often just to talk, even if we couldn't see each other during the week.

However, other aspects of our relationship troubled me. Even after we had dated for almost a year, Jay refused to introduce me to his family or even tell them about me. I longed to meet the family of the person I loved.

"Why won't you let me meet your family?" I asked.

"I'm just a really private person," he said.

"Is it our spiritual differences?" I asked him.

Jay was raised with some misconceptions about Catholics. Even though I no longer practiced Catholicism, maybe his family wouldn't accept that I was raised Catholic.

"No, that's not it," he said.

Still, Jay was a conservative Christian, viewing my studies and the books on my shelf with suspicion. My collection hosted an array of sacred scriptures and wisdom literature, ranging from different versions of the Bible, Buddhist texts, the Quran, the Tao Te Ching, the Rig Vedas, and the Bhagavad Gita. He knew I studied comparative worldviews and philosophies in graduate school, but I could never tell him I didn't affiliate myself with a particular faith. I found wisdom and beauty in all the world religions and felt I could learn something valuable from all of them. Unlike so many people around me, I *wanted* to broaden my mind. I wondered why anyone would limit oneself to a single philosophy or religion. I wanted to know a God or the Universe stripped of all the labels and dogmas.

In my mind, many paths lead to the light. One does not have to identify with a particular faith or religion to have a relationship with God or the divine. If we're lucky, we believe in something that contributes to our happiness, health, peace of mind, and sense of purpose. It doesn't matter whether we experience a deeper connection to the Universe through prayer, meditation, nature, service, movement, or art. What matters is that we see dignity in all human beings and help alleviate their suffering. Likewise, we allow others to explore and experience the divine in whatever form resonates most with them, even if it's completely different from our own. People and their beliefs do not matter to me as long as they are kind and decent. I am friends with adherents of all different religions and enjoy the multiplicity of perspectives I encounter.

While I am unbound to organized religion, I feel most at home in the Eastern traditions of Buddhism and Taoism. Jay had enough difficulty accepting my Catholic upbringing. How could I tell him what I really believed? I feared if I did, it would end our relationship.

Jay, on the other hand, had no desire to search beyond what he had been taught and wanted a woman who shared his beliefs. Essentially, he wanted his future partner to be a Baptist Republican housewife.

"Women like that are a dime a dozen in Oklahoma," I said, laughing. "What are you doing with me? I am none of those things."

He chuckled. "That's a good question."

Jay had found one of the few spiritually open, progressive feminists in Oklahoma. His mother was a conservative Christian homemaker, providing the only model he knew. I like to think I opened his mind to other possibilities.

"It's a good thing nothing bad ever happened to your dad," I said. "My mother had no choice but to work outside our home when my dad died. Women need to have job skills. They have to be able to support themselves financially."

"I guess I had never thought about that," Jay said.

More important than our spiritual differences, Jay wouldn't tell me he loved me. "I care so much about you," he would say, which left me to conclude he wasn't serious about me. Nonetheless, I couldn't bear the idea of breaking up with him.

* * *

ON A TYPICAL MORNING IN February, I received a heartbreaking call from my sister Kelley.

"John just died," she cried.

"What?" I was stunned. John had been a faithful parent to me for over twenty years. "How?"

"He had a heart attack out in the field this morning," she said. I could hear my mother's heart-wrenching sobs in the background.

I dropped the receiver and screamed, "Noooooo!" The agony of losing my father and now John flooded my entire being. Grief and shock, as deep as a well, tore open inside of me.

Jay squeezed me and said, "I love you so much."

The only time Jay told me he loved me. I knew how he meant it—as a human, not someone he was in love with.

I held on to Jay. "I have to go to my mom!" I exclaimed.

I couldn't bear watching my mother lose her husband a second time. I wished so much I could take away her pain. And to lose my second father. It was too much.

On top of it all, Jay said nothing about attending the funeral, and I had to ask him to accompany me at least to John's wake. I needed his support. That I had to ask him did not sit well with me. Only in his twenties, perhaps he didn't understand, having never experienced the untimely death of a loved one, or maybe he didn't know how to handle my pain.

In any case, John's death reminded me how quickly life can vanish. As much as it aggrieved me, I broke up with Jay. I knew he didn't view me as a life partner.

"You don't accept me for who I am," I told him.

"Yes, I do," he said. "You're a wonderful person."

"But I'm not what you want, and I can't be what you want," I told him.

I wasn't a conservative Oklahoma girl who wanted to stay home and have babies. I longed to travel the world, explore diverse cultures, and learn about people who are different from me. Why did men see that as a shortcoming? When would I find a man who loved my open mind and free spirit?

Jay and I clutched each other and cried the rest of the night. I loved him and couldn't imagine myself without him.

For the next two years, I mourned my lost love. Jay and I stayed in touch, but I missed his physical presence, affection, and sweetness. He showed me that all men aren't trying to harm or use me, that all men won't abandon me. And he made me feel beautiful.

"At least you had a lovely experience," Sister Sheila said.

Despite the heartbreak, yes, it was a gift.

CHAPTER 17

Going the Distance

Oklahoma City Memorial Marathon
2011

ON A FEBRUARY EVENING, I received a call from my sister-in-law. She was crying.

She took a deep breath and said, "Jeff has been in an accident."

My big brother. My mind flashed to my dad's accident and contemplated the worst.

"Is he alive?" I asked, fearing her answer.

"Yes," she said. "He's been taken to the ER."

I sighed with relief. "Thank God!"

That night, my family and I rushed to the Dallas area where he lived. Jeff had been in a cycling collision and broke his back. He had just been taken into emergency surgery.

I cried and cried. Partially paralyzed, he would most likely never run or cycle again—activities he loved. I had just run with him a few months before—the one and only time we ran together. I had started running again the year before to improve my fitness, even running a half marathon for the first time.

After my brother's accident, I realized our abilities could be taken away anytime. I had no more excuses. I vowed to train for and run the Oklahoma City Memorial Marathon in his honor. This race, known as the Run to Remember, was especially meaningful to me, as it commemorated the 168 people killed in the Oklahoma City bombing.

* * *

AFTER MONTHS OF TRAINING, I paced the floor of the clinic, awaiting the doctor's diagnosis. With an excruciating ache in my right knee, I couldn't run more than a few feet.

"Well, you have stressed your knee," he said.

"What about running the marathon?" I asked him. "It's three weeks away."

"Oh, you won't be running with that," he said. "You need to stay off your knee."

My heart sank.

As I left the clinic, tears poured from my eyes. I had trained so hard for the last three months. I had worked out with a personal trainer twice per week, logged twenty-plus mile runs, and taken yoga classes. For what? This race was supposed to be for my brother.

Then I remembered what I had learned from the State track meet my sophomore year of high school exactly twenty years ago. *Don't give up just because of an injury. Find a way.*

First, I had to talk to the right people, the ones who would figure out *how* I could run, not *if* I could run.

My personal trainer reassured me. "Don't worry. Your knee is just a little mad at you right now. Rest it and see how you feel in three weeks."

I knew I couldn't quit training altogether. Rather than running, I worked out on low-impact exercise equipment, did yoga, and continued with my personal trainer.

Two days before the marathon, my knee still smarted, and I had to make a decision. While I didn't mind hurting, I didn't want to permanently damage my knee, either.

"You should see Dr. Tom," one of my friends told me. "He's the medical director for the Oklahoma City Memorial Marathon and a runner himself. He'll tell you how you can run."

I immediately scheduled an appointment with Dr. Tom. A wiry man in his seventies, I could tell he had run thousands of miles and would run thousands more if he could. He grasped my leg on his exam table, bending it forward, backward, and side to side.

"Where does it hurt?" he asked.

"Outside of my right knee."

"Oh, you can run," he said. "It's just bursitis."

"You mean I won't permanently damage my knee?" I asked him.

"No, you'll be fine," he said. "It will just hurt. I can give you a shot of steroids in your knee if you like."

I considered what he said and didn't like the thought of having a needle injected into my knee.

"I'll just tough it out," I told him.

"Let's see your shoes," he said.

He took out my insoles and taped some padding on them. Then he stretched a piece of tape across my right forefoot.

"Now, let's get your shoes back on, so I can see you walk in them."

I strode down the hall by his office.

"How does that feel?" he asked.

"Better!" I said.

"That tape will correct your gait and take some of the stress off that knee."

I was elated! I could run after all.

* * *

THE MORNING OF THE MARATHON, I peered out my car at the horde of people. Dressed only in black tights and a blue long-sleeve Dri-FIT shirt, I glanced at the sky and saw clouds creeping in. Just a thirty percent chance of rain was forecast today. Surely, it wasn't about to rain.

A second later, drops pooled on the windshield.

"Seriously?" I muttered.

I hadn't brought any waterproof apparel. Checking my clock, I knew I had no time to go home and retrieve rain gear. I would have to grind through it. At least it wasn't supposed to get cold.

As I joined the thousands of runners at the starting line, the clouds that had been taunting us from afar drifted over our heads and began sprinkling. I jogged in place, my teeth chattering from nerves and shivers. Not running in the last three weeks, I didn't know how my knee would fare, but I would give it my all.

When the runners and I took off, my knee started throbbing from the pounding pavement. *Hang in there,* I told it. *You have a marathon to run*. I burrowed into the pack of runners, and the tension seemed to ease. With all the marathoners, half-marathoners, and 5K runners moving en masse, the first few miles felt transcendent! It was like we were pulling each other along.

After the marathoners split off, however, the crowd dwindled, leaving me alone to ponder my predicament. Soaked to the bone, a cold gust of air pelted me. *Did I just imagine that?*

Hail!

"You've got to be fuckin' kidding me!" I muttered. "No one said anything about hail! Damn Oklahoma forecasts are always wrong!"

Frozen pellets hammered my head and hands, bouncing off the ground in a wild tap dance.

I needed a beacon. *Yes, the marathon route goes near my sister's house!* I called Kelley and told her I was approaching.

"You're calling me while running a marathon?" she asked.

"Sure, why not? It's not like I have anything else to do."

"Okay, we'll be out there!" she said.

Seeing Kelley and my eight-year-old niece Jaclyn cheer me on at mile 17 gave me the boost I needed—but it was short-lived. At mile 18, I started wearing down. Progress was slow and painful, and I could no longer feel my hands or legs. The numbness may have worked out in my favor, however. With my legs deadening from the cold, I could no longer feel the pain in my knee.

At mile 20, my blood sugar was depleting, my energy was sagging, and my back muscles were verging on shutdown. I had never run in more miserable conditions. When the hail eventually ceased, cold sheets of rain pounded the pavement, the spring colors disappearing into a surreal wash of gray.

This was it. I was entering unknown territory. I had never run more than twenty miles at one time in my life. Every marathoner knows the race comes down to the last 6.2 miles. Each mile after 20 becomes exponentially more difficult than the previous one and lasts infinitely longer. Well-meaning spectators shout, "You're almost there!" at mile 23. They have no idea.

With each step, I didn't know how I would continue. I was dying from fatigue and about to drop. I knew if I were to stop, I would freeze. Each time I thought about quitting, I thought of my brother and remembered why I was running. With deepening resolve, I wiped the merciless raindrops from my eyes and kept pushing forward, knowing the sooner I finished, the sooner I could doff the cold, wet clothes.

At last, I made the final turn onto Broadway Avenue at mile 26, the finish line in sight! I tried to give my legs one final kick—only for them to cramp up. My electrolytes had depleted, and I would be lucky to walk. Hobbling over the finish line, I heard, "Go, Hollie!"

I turned to the side and saw my mother and her boyfriend Bob, the best sight I had seen in hours! They had come down in this wretched weather to watch me finish. As soon as I crossed the finish line, I sank into my mom's arms.

"I'm so proud of you!" she said.

Mom handed me a snack, but I couldn't grasp it. Hypothermia had set in, and my motor skills had disappeared with my waning energy. While I was famished, I just wanted to escape the cold rain and get something hot to drink. One of the race officials put a finisher's medal around my neck, but I felt so miserable, I couldn't celebrate my triumph. I merely nodded at him.

Hours later, after I had thawed out and changed into dry clothes, I was able to revel in the victory. *Did I really just do that?*

Of course, I didn't "win" anything. Out of twenty thousand runners, I was not the best runner—not even close. But I gained something even more critical. My love for my sport returned. And it wasn't based on winning championships or making anyone else happy. It was the pure euphoria of the experience, of pushing myself farther than I thought I could go.

Not surprisingly, once a runner completes a marathon, the

crown achievement of any distance runner, she has either one of two thoughts: *I am never doing this again*, or *When can I do it again?*

As crazy as it was, I wanted to do it again.

Part Four

TOUCHING THE VOID

CHAPTER 18
Flashback

Oklahoma City
June 2016

I WALKED INTO THE STORE and saw him—Boy #1. I hadn't seen him in almost thirty years. Afraid he would see me, I changed course to enter the other door, so our paths wouldn't cross.

Anxiety seized me. *Hollie, he can't hurt you now,* I told myself.

The unsettling vision jarred me. *Go to the food bar. Get some food. Check out. Get out of here as fast as possible.* I tried to shut the images out of my mind as I drove to Dr. Tom's summer running party.

But seeing *him* awakened a long-dormant part of my memory. A crack appeared in the dam I had built to block the flow of unwanted emotions and memories into my consciousness. Now, through that tiny slit, they seeped in. I sprang into high alert, frantically trying to seal the opening, so that everything could return to normal.

When I met my friends at the gathering, I managed to hide behind a veneer of false cheerfulness, but when I got home, the images continued to pierce through.

The next day, I texted my therapist. For days I was rattled. Anywhere I went, I saw Boy #1, yet I didn't see him. *It's not him,* I assured myself. *Just a guy who could pass for him with a cursory glance.* But I had to be prepared if it was.

* * *

I SAT ON THE COUCH in my therapist's office. Ever since I saw Boy #1, flashbacks of the assault terrorized me. Stashed away were all the harrowing memories my mind wanted to forget. Most of the time, I could suppress them, but in moments of distress, or for no apparent reason, the box snapped open, all its contents scattering.

"I have nightmares and wake up shaking and can't breathe," I told her. "When I think of other hard things I've gone through, like a breakup or even someone dying, the pain eases with time, but this is different," I said.

"It's like a fire that keeps burning," she said.

"Exactly. No matter what I try, it won't leave me."

"Do you try to avoid anything that reminds you of it?" she asked.

"Well, yeah." I squirmed in my seat and gulped hard. "I can hardly stand to think about it."

"It sounds like you have all the symptoms of PTSD," she said.

"Really?" I asked, mulling over what she said. *Post-traumatic stress disorder*. I knew war veterans and first responders suffered from it, but me?

A psychologist in her mid-thirties, my therapist was a trauma specialist. She explained that anyone who has experienced a shocking, frightening, or dangerous event could develop PTSD. It can include sexual violence, childhood abuse, physical assaults, violent threats, accidents, natural disasters, acts of terror, active military combat, and the sudden loss of a loved one—anything that threatens one's basic sense of safety. While nearly everyone experiences a range of reactions after a traumatic event, most people recover from the initial symptoms naturally. In contrast, those with PTSD feel stressed or alarmed even when they are no longer in danger. Any reminder of the event may trigger the rapid appearance of recurrent, unwanted, and distressing memories—as if the event is happening right now.

When my therapist told me what the symptoms are, I was astounded.

Intrusive memories. Having recurrent, unwanted, and distressing memories of the traumatic event, reliving the event as if it were happening again, having upsetting dreams or nightmares about the event.

Avoidance. Avoiding thoughts or conversations about the traumatic event; circumventing places, activities, or people that remind you of the event.

Negative changes in thinking and mood. Having negative thoughts about yourself, other people, or the world; harboring hopelessness about the future; having lapses in memory regarding important aspects of the event.

Changes in physical and emotional reactions. Getting easily startled or frightened, remaining on guard for danger, having trouble sleeping and concentrating, suffering from overwhelming guilt or shame.

As I absorbed what she said, I couldn't deny she described everything I had been experiencing or had experienced so many times in the past. Now it all made sense. The nightmares, flashbacks, and intrusive memories from the sexual assaults. The constant fear I would lose people important to me. I wasn't going crazy then—at least I could tell myself that when I wasn't triggered.

"There are two types of therapy we can try," she said.

"Prolonged exposure or cognitive processing therapy."

I chose the latter, which helps clients learn how to challenge and modify unhelpful beliefs related to the trauma. The goal was to create a new understanding of the traumatic events so that they reduced their ongoing negative effects on my life.

To start my treatment for PTSD, my therapist asked me to write down what happened to me—the details of the assault. As I began to type it, unsettling thoughts invaded my mind. *No, I don't want to think about that.* Instead, I wrote about the conditions that set me up for what happened—how I ended up alone with the boys, how breaking my jaws affected my self-confidence, how I had just started puberty the year before. I read my account aloud to my therapist, thinking I did well.

My therapist frowned and said, "This isn't meant to be a criticism, but I noticed you didn't mention anything about the perpetrators."

"Oh, no, I guess I didn't."

After a few seconds of silence, she asked, "What part did they play? Can you tell me what happened?"

I shifted in my seat.

"I don't think I can," I said, my voice shaking.

I stared at the floor and started trembling. Alarming thoughts cascaded through my mind. *Me trying to run away. Them ripping my blouse. Them pinning me to the ground. Me lying there afterward.* I couldn't verbalize the images overtaking my head.

"I tried to make them stop," I said, breaking into tears.

"How did it start?"

"I don't remember."

"What did they do?"

"I don't remember," I snapped.

No, I *did* remember. More accurately, I should have said, "I don't want to remember."

I looked back at what I had written. Without recognizing it, I blamed myself for what happened. *Isn't that what I have been doing for the last twenty-eight years?*

"Blaming yourself is what's keeping the fire burning," my therapist said.

"Yeah, I feel like I have to atone for what happened, that I have to prove I'm a good person," I said.

"So, you've given yourself a life sentence," she said.

I sighed. "Yeah, I guess so. The one thing I can't reconcile in my mind was how I felt physically."

"It doesn't matter whether you felt physically aroused. You didn't give consent, and you couldn't have."

No, I never gave them permission, but still . . .

My therapist continued. "At thirteen years old, you are not capable of giving consent. Your mind isn't developed enough. That's why there are laws against it."

I thought she said that to make me feel better. I still didn't believe it. I assumed I was to blame.

* * *

I SPENT THE NEXT SEVERAL weeks with my therapist trying to unlearn everything I had told myself.

Men just want to use me.

I don't deserve love.

Any romantic relationship I have is doomed to fail.

I am too broken to have a healthy romantic relationship.

If I let a man get close to me, he will hurt me.

I deserve what happened to me.

Most men want to hurt me.

"Have you ever heard of the just-world phenomenon?" my therapist asked.

"No, I don't think so," I said.

"As children, we're taught that the world is a fair and just place. That was reinforced with the ideas like Santa Claus—if you're a good boy or girl, Santa Claus will bring you presents. People, particularly children, need to protect their view of the world as a safe and fair place. When something harmful or unjust happens, the child either has to admit the world is *not* safe and just, like they have been told, or that they did something to deserve it.

"When you were assaulted, you either had to let go of the idea that the world is not safe, or believe you were at fault and did something to deserve what happened," my therapist explained.

On an intellectual level, it made perfect sense to me, but I still couldn't let go of the belief that the assaults were my responsibility.

CHAPTER 19
Unmasked

Oklahoma City
June – August 2016

MY MOTHER COULD ALWAYS SENSE when something was off with me. On the phone a few days later, she asked, "Honey, what's wrong?"

I started to weep. For a moment, the strong, independent woman I had become was gone. All the roles had been stripped away, leaving behind the young girl crying under her covers, who wanted to shield her mother from more pain, who was consumed with guilt and shame for the role she played in what happened to her.

"I don't know if I could ever tell you," I said.

"Oh, honey, you can tell me anything."

Maybe this was it. Maybe it was time to tell her. I took a deep breath, summoning all the courage I could.

And I told her . . .

"I always knew something happened to you," she said. "Why didn't you tell me?"

"I was too ashamed," I said, "and I didn't want you to blame yourself. Plus, I had written that story, and you were so upset about it. I thought you would be even more ashamed of me."

Mom sighed. "Oh, honey. I completely overreacted to that story. It was clever and funny. I reacted the way I did because that principal made a big deal out of it. And I was so worried about what was going on with Kelley."

I wish I had known that at the time.

"Girls always blame themselves for this stuff," she said. "It wasn't your fault. I tried to get you to talk to me, but you wouldn't open up."

"I don't remember that."

My mother's tone transformed from concern to anger. "Your daddy and John would want to kill those boys for doing that to you."

Maybe she does understand.

As her emotions continued to shift, Mom changed her inflection again. "Well, honey, that happened so long ago. You can't let it interfere with your life now. There's no point in still thinking about it. Look at what a wonderful life you have."

"Mom, if I could turn it off like a switch, I would. I found out I have PTSD," I said.

"Oh, you don't have PTSD."

"How would you know? You haven't lived in my head for the last forty years. Do you even know what it is?"

"Of course. I had it after my wreck as a teenager."

"Then why is it hard to understand I would have it after what happened to me?"

Steam rose from my head. I knew my mother was trying to be helpful, but minimizing my experience and invalidating my reality only incensed me, and I knew further conversation was pointless.

"I have to go now," I said.

"I love you, and I just don't want to see you unhappy," she said.

I wish she could see how hard I was trying.

* * *

OVER THE NEXT FEW WEEKS, interactions between my mother and me were strained. She understood me in some ways, but in other ways, I was as alien to her as the smartphone she struggled to operate every day. I concluded it was better not to discuss my troubles with her, to pretend everything was normal, just like she wanted. Despite our efforts, the charade could last only so long.

One night, my mother called me around nine p.m.

"I have something to tell you," she said.

"Yeah, what?" I asked.

"He is going to be at the birthday party," she said.

Boy #1.

"What?" I exclaimed. "He can't come. I have to say something."

"No, don't say anything. It will ruin the birthday celebration," she said.

I couldn't believe what I was hearing. Not "ruining" my relative's birthday was more important than my family hanging out with someone who repeatedly assaulted me. A sudden rage coursed through me. A fury and anguish I couldn't express in words. I hurled my cell phone on the floor and unleashed a primal scream.

In shock at the raw emotion, my mother asked, "Are you done?" when I picked up the phone.

"No, I won't be silent anymore!" I screamed.

"Don't say *anything,*" Mom repeated.

The hell I am.

"I have kept quiet for almost thirty years! If that guy is going to be there, I won't go. I can't be in the same room with him," I said.

It was the first time I stood up to my mother and defied what she had taught me. My mother, who was my everything, the person dearest to me. Sometimes I didn't know where she ended and where I began. In this instance, I knew.

I not only told my relative, but other members of my family.

Telling them was just as wounding. While they were sympathetic, they told me I needed to move on and let go of the past. It happened so long ago. It couldn't have been that bad. The boys were kids too.

Ultimately, my relative was unwilling to disinvite his friend who had assaulted me. My family was willing to hang out with Boy #1, knowing what he did to me. Maybe it was easier for them to believe I was overreacting than to believe this person did something so hurtful and damaging to me. They didn't know I had tried to suppress my pain for years, which, despite my efforts, cut close to the surface, the memories like splinters lodged under my skin.

The hurt and betrayal cut me to the core. Avoiding an uncomfortable situation was more important to them than supporting me. Maybe they didn't want to believe this seemingly ordinary guy did something horrific to me.

I didn't speak to my mother, whom I usually spoke with every day, for about a week. I was too gutted. She supported me in all my other hardships. Why not in this situation? In one of the worst trials I have ever had to deal with?

When I spoke to her again, I asked her, "Do you all not believe me?"

"No, we believe you. You have to understand we need time to adjust."

I couldn't get over my family choosing to hang out with this guy, knowing what he did. In my mind, they chose him over me. He had traumatized me to the point I was still struggling with the aftermath nearly thirty years later. If it were simply a matter of letting it go, I would have done so already.

Worse yet, my mother didn't get it, and it seemed like she didn't *want* to get it—which devastated me. Mom was the closest person in the world to me. I was not only injured from the original incident and still carrying the open wound, but my family's reaction added another layer of injury. All I wanted was for them to see it and hold it with me.

My family clearly didn't understand the depth of the impact on me. While they meant well, dismissing my experience and telling me to move on made it worse. Perhaps they felt powerless, not knowing how to help me. Perhaps I reminded them of their own traumas they had sealed away for years. All they had to do was say they were here with me, and that I wasn't facing it alone.

My therapist told me not telling anyone right after the assault occurred had put me at higher risk for developing PTSD. Without access to the appropriate resources, treatments, and social networks to build back my sense of safety and help me feel less isolated, I didn't heal properly. That's what I was trying to change.

Furthermore, my revelation was inconsistent with what my family and most people knew about me. Many people with PTSD are high-functioning, competent people who can still persevere—until they have an episode or a flashback, and family members cannot make sense of it. They don't understand that the brain gets hijacked and stuck in the past, reliving the traumatic events. The brain loses touch with the present and believes the trauma is happening in real time. My family didn't understand I had been concealing and stifling my trauma for decades. I was exhausted from wearing the mask and letting the trauma consume me on the inside. I wanted to heal.

Moreover, with severe physical injuries, no one expects someone to rebound instantly without going through appropriate treatment. For example, as of this writing, I am recovering from breaking and dislocating both of my elbows in a cycling accident. I will have to go through hundreds of hours of physical therapy for the next few months to restore my full functionality and range of motion. And even then, I will always feel the effects of the injury. No one would expect my bones to mend immediately without any outside medical treatment or effort from me. No one would tell me just to "get over it" and "move on." Why do people expect instant healing with mental and emotional trauma and not with severe physical trauma?

Part of the reason is they can't *see* emotional trauma—but perhaps it goes even deeper. By acknowledging that someone is a victim, they would need to concede that they, too, could be victims. People don't like to think about themselves becoming the targets of a violent crime, so when they hear about an event such as an assault or a rape, they may try to blame the victim's behavior. This allows people to believe they can avoid becoming victims of crime just by avoiding past victims' actions. By blaming victims for their misfortunes, they can ease their own anxiety and avoid facing their own vulnerability, and perhaps their belief that the world is just and fair. Still, it is an injustice or misfortune, no different than someone suffering the effects of a natural disaster or a mugging. In those cases, people don't ask what they were wearing or what they did to bring it on themselves. I wished more people could see that.

CHAPTER 20

Triggered

Eureka Springs, Arkansas
October 2016

AFTER THE UPHEAVAL OF THE last few months, I needed to get away. A solo hiking trip to Arkansas to enjoy the fall foliage seemed like the perfect remedy.

On my final day in Arkansas, I stopped in Eureka Springs, a Victorian resort village nestled in the Ozarks. A popular tourist destination, its steep, tight-winding streets were packed with cars and pedestrians. I drove around for twenty minutes, trying to locate a place to park. The best I could find was an empty spot in a dirt lot behind a café. While not an actual parking space, it would do, and I hoped my car wouldn't get towed.

After having lunch in one of the other downtown cafés, I returned a couple of hours later to find a car parked behind mine. *Crap, I can't get out.* I walked around the vehicle to see if the owner was inside. From a distance, I heard, "Get away from my car." Not knowing it was directed at me, again, I heard, "I *said* get away from my car!"

A bald man in his thirties, muscular and tattooed, closed in on me. His face inches from mine, with a forehead creased beyond his years, he screamed, "What makes you think you can park there! That's my spot!"

My eyes widened, and I stepped back. I tried to remain calm. "That's not even a real parking place. How can it be yours?"

"That's where I park for work! Why would you park there?"

"There was no other place to park," I said. "How was I supposed to know it was *your* spot? There's no sign."

"You are the most selfish bitch I have ever met!"

A young woman, whom I assumed to be his significant other, stood by his side. I looked at her like, *Are you going to let him talk to me like that?*

"There's no reason to get verbally abusive," I said. "I am about to leave, and you can park your car there. Will you please move your car?"

"No!"

"You can't just trap my car here. Please let me leave," I said.

He crept toward me again and shouted, "You should have thought about that before you parked there! You are the most selfish person I have ever met!"

I trembled. "Please, just move your car and let me leave."

I cast an imploring look at the woman beside him.

"Come on," she told him.

At long last, the thug moved his car.

I drove off as fast as I could. Once I reached a safe distance from town, my shoulders dropped, releasing their mounting tension, and I bawled. *What just happened?* I had traveled all over the world and never felt like someone would physically attack me. *Eureka Springs of all freakin' places! One of the safest places in the world!*

So I had thought. I pressed on without stopping, trying to put as much space between the thug and me as possible. The incident forced me to acknowledge what I didn't want to accept: It is risky for a woman to travel alone, no matter where she goes.

No way could I tell my mother what happened. It would give her more reason to worry when I traveled. Instead, I called her boyfriend, who was an attorney. Bob, a gentle, quiet intellectual, was sharp-witted and could keep a clear head.

"What can I do?" I asked him. I envisaged him taking a puff from his pipe and stroking his silver-gray hair and well-groomed mustache.

"You could call the Eureka Springs Police Department and file a police report," he said.

Call the police! Of course! In my distress and panic, it hadn't even occurred to me.

"Do you think I should do that?" I asked.

"Well, you just want to make sure he can't track you down," Bob said.

"Okay, I will think about it. Please don't tell my mom."

I shuddered. What if I gave my name to the police, they told him who I was, and he did find me? Ultimately, I determined it was worth the risk. I didn't want him to think he could get away with treating women like that.

I called the police department and reported everything I could remember. I described what the man looked like, what car he drove, where he usually parked, and the place he worked. I asked that they not reveal my name to him.

I have no idea if the police identified or spoke to him. I could only hope they did, and he would think twice about threatening a single woman again.

I was shaken for several weeks. *What would I have done if he attacked me?* I wouldn't have been able to defend myself. I was already agitated from seeing Boy #1 and now this. I had never liked guns nor desired to own a firearm, but did I need to get one?

A week later, I met Mom and Bob for breakfast.

When Mom went to the restroom, Bob whispered, "Did you call the police?"

"Yes," I said.

Bob was so sweet to help me. While reporting the thug to the police helped me restore some power over the situation, one question continued to nag me. *Will I ever feel safe traveling by myself again?*

CHAPTER 21

Epiphany

Oklahoma City
November 2016

MY ROOM WAS HOT AND stuffy, but I was shaking. November. That dreaded time of year. The month I was assaulted twenty-eight years ago. I rose from my bed, turned on the living room light, and walked over to the mirror. A softer, younger image of myself reflected in the glass. My brown eyes stared back at me.

I am Hollie. I am forty-one. I am at my house in Oklahoma City. I am not getting assaulted.

That's what my therapist taught me to do—ground myself and remind myself where I was. Tears flooded my eyes as I remembered that horrific day twenty-eight years ago with a clarity I hadn't before.

My body quivering, I texted my therapist. I needed to tell her—in all the ghastly detail.

No matter how hard I tried, the past kept coming back, and alongside it, the pain. The memory of those afternoons long ago dwelled inside me, along with the guilt, shame, and self-loathing. The memories danced in front of my eyes. Something long trapped was trying to break its way free.

For years I had tried to suppress the memories. To deliberately recall them exhausted and frightened me. The layer of fog had protected me all these years. Of course, I remembered major fragments of what happened, but to part the clouds, to find the missing pieces, opened an old wound that had never been given the chance to fully heal. I couldn't shake the feeling that the assault was somehow my fault. Worse yet, I felt like I had been betrayed by my own body. I needed something to show me the way out of the quandary that had tormented me since I was thirteen.

The following month, I attended a workshop at the local YWCA to learn how to empower and advocate for women who were victims of sexual and domestic abuse. A social worker in my class talked about child sexual abuse and how adult abusers take advantage of children's bodily reactions to make them think they wanted or enjoyed the abuse.

I whipped around to her and asked, "Is that common? That kids report feeling aroused?"

"Yes," she said, "and I tell them that is what their body is designed to do. And that doesn't mean that they wanted it to happen."

Her explanation stunned me. There it was—the critical piece I had been missing—the secret abuse victims don't openly discuss.

As I learned throughout the training, involuntary physiological responses do not constitute consent. Similarly, one cannot control getting goose bumps when they are cold or perspiring when they are exposed to heat. It just happens. Furthermore, anyone who is underage, intoxicated, incapacitated by drugs or alcohol, asleep, or unconscious cannot give explicit consent. Likewise, if one agrees to an activity under pressure, intimidation, or threat, it's not consensual because they cannot extend it freely. Unequal power dynamics, resulting in sexual activity with an employee or student, also are not considered consensual.

That was a game changer for me.

With the epiphany came liberation, but also a difficult truth. That meant I had been a victim, and I didn't want to be one. Admitting victimhood isn't easy. If I were a victim once, it means I could be one again. In a way, it was much easier to believe I somehow deserved what happened, so I could control it, rather than believe I was subject to other humans' random, malicious actions. Acknowledging someone could assault me again, like the man in Eureka Springs, was petrifying.

In my next session with my therapist, I said what I had never been able to say before. "I was sexually abused."

Only then could I release it.

Sexual abuse doesn't just happen between adults and children, but between children, as in my case.

With the realization that I wasn't responsible for the abuse, I became angry at my schools' teaching. It's not enough to teach children to say "no" or "stop." As apparent in my case, that doesn't always work. It's just as important, if not *more* important, to teach *children* to stop when someone tells them, "Stop."

Doing so is more critical since our culture instills contradictory messages. I have spoken to men who have told me they were taught that a woman always says "no" at first because she doesn't want to look like a "slut," but she really means "yes."

"Oh no," I told them. "When a woman says 'no,' 'stop,' or expresses *any* hesitation, you back off immediately."

Was that what the boys who assaulted me thought? I have often asked myself what made them attack me. They had to learn it from somewhere. Perhaps they learned it from viewing porn, where scenes of non-consensual sex abound. After all, most porn does not depict healthy, loving, and respectful interactions or relationships, much less what consent or agency looks like.

If parents discuss sex with their sons at all, they generally limit conversations to "don't get her pregnant" lectures. Parents most likely don't explain the laws to them, if they even know what they are; therefore, boys don't understand that consent needs to be informed, enthusiastic, sober, ongoing, and given freely. A rapist or assailant is usually not a bad guy in the bushes with a gun. They are everyday people who may not understand that a partner can withdraw consent *at any time*, and that consenting to *some* sexual acts is not agreeing to *all* sexual acts.

To that end, why did no one in my schools talk about the difference between consensual sexual contact and sexual abuse? Maybe if all schools had had age-appropriate discussions, the boys who assaulted me wouldn't have thought it was okay to do what they did. The only occasion one of my schools discussed rape, sexual assault, and consent was when I was a senior in high school. By that time, it was most likely too late. How many students had been assaulted by then? Whatever the case, I knew this had to change.

No wonder I hadn't been able to reconcile sexual assault and consensual sexual activity feeling physically similar, especially since my first experience was non-consensual. I have since learned about "somatic flashbacks" or "body memories," in which the body physically reexperiences the sensations of the trauma, along with the guilt, shame, and disgust. To this day, if I have a physical relationship with a guy, memories of the abuse often invade my mind, and I have to remind myself that I am no longer in the traumatic experience. PTSD is not just in one's head. It lives in the body if untreated.

My schools, in retrospect, seemed more concerned with maintaining "chastity," as if that is some veritable honor. Why did no one discuss the importance of consent, rather or secondary to discussions about the sinfulness of sex outside of marriage, masturbation, and the Church's stance against the use of birth control? Instead of the focus on "sin," why not emphasize the importance of not causing others harm, whether that is using someone for sex or sexually violating someone?

No, I didn't deserve what happened to me, and God was not punishing me.

So many people attribute everything to God, including the most horrific calamities, and try to explain the reason behind God's inexplicably unmerciful actions. I don't believe what happened to me was because of God or some cosmic design. God, the Universe, or whatever term one prefers to use, doesn't do bad things to people and doesn't punish people. People do bad things to people. The world may not be inherently fair or just, but we can create a more just world for our fellow humans through our own agency. If we see an injustice, like errant messaging around sex and sexual assault, we can help correct it.

For so many years, I thought I had to be a "good" Catholic to redress what I thought I had done wrong. Even years after I plotted my own spiritual path, the Church's teachings around sex held fast. Now I no longer care about being a "good" Catholic, a "good" Christian, or adhering to any other man-formulated religious dogma. I care only about being a good *human*.

Even my epiphany, however, could not silence the echoes of November or quash the events that continued to pull me down.

CHAPTER 22
Bluer Than Indigo

Oklahoma City
November 2016

THROUGHOUT THE NIGHT, I TOSSED and turned, my back and belly slick with sweat. I woke up disoriented and thirsty, trying to shake off the haunting memories. My throat felt parched and dry, like dead leaves.

Disentangling myself from the wet sheets, I fumbled to the kitchen, hoping the light, airy room would rouse me from the dark shadows that engulfed me. I opened the blinds and flinched at the glare of the morning sun. By all appearances, it was a lovely autumn day. I guzzled my glass of water, wondering what I was going to do. For the first time in my life, I didn't see a way out of the pain. In all my hardships and traumas, no matter how bleak they had been, I never wanted my life to end. I always knew I would eventually feel okay.

This time was different.

I want to die, I thought.

No, I don't really want to die. I just want the pain to stop.

The thoughts were spontaneous and intrusive—and they frightened me.

Should I tell someone? No. I didn't plan on doing anything and didn't want to alarm anyone. But the ruminations still terrorized me.

Most of all, I felt ashamed. I had this fantastic life. *What right do I have to feel the way I do?* I was the one who made people laugh and uplifted them. I didn't want to burden anyone or show this side of myself.

Hoping to find comfort, I scrolled through my photos on Facebook—the races, my voyages, my friends. I stared blankly at them, trying to remember what joy feels like. Instead, I felt nothing but emptiness. How could reminiscences from recent photos seem so distant, while recollections of the sexual trauma feel as raw as they were nearly 30 years ago? I set down my phone and lay on my sofa. As I reached for my glass of water, the picture displayed on my phone caught my eye. *Jack.* It was my nephew and me after we had run a race a couple of years earlier. *I could never leave him or any of my nieces.* I had to make it through for them.

I picked up my phone and googled how to manage suicidal ideations. Remember, there is always a way out, a website said. *But I don't see the way out.*

Casting my thoughts aside as much as I could, I rose and turned to the task at hand. My Toastmasters friends were coming over in an hour for Thanksgiving dinner. I had no choice but to get ready.

* * *

MY FRIENDS ARRIVED WITH FOOD and drinks. Sharing their laughter and good cheer roused a warmth I hadn't experienced in several weeks. I snapped back to my merry self and played the gracious hostess. My friends would no doubt be shocked at the deep melancholy that lurked beneath, that I was hanging on by a thread. If only they knew.

After my friends left, I felt lighter. They had kindled a hopeful glimmer in me, and the embers carried me through the night.

Yet I awoke the following day with a heaviness that deepened the hole in my heart. Still, I had to get up and go to work. Despite the sun shining, tears rushed to my eyes, discoloring the world into an ugly place. I felt trapped in the dark winter of my life, and I couldn't find the escape route. At the office, I heard my coworkers' voices, but I was slow to process them.

While at work, I called my friend Mandy. *Maybe I should tell her.* But she was about to leave the country. *I can't tell her now.*

Election Day had been the last straw. The President-elect was dominating the news with the uncovered *Access Hollywood* tape in which he said, "Grab them by the pussy." With everything I was processing, this revelation was devastating to me. It wasn't just what the President-elect had said. After all, everyone has said harmful words at times, and people can express remorse and change their behaviors. It's that so many people around me thought it was okay to say that. I couldn't believe people, including ones I loved, still voted for him, knowing he had twenty sexual assault accusers and was reported to have walked in on underage pageant contestants as young as fifteen undressing. It showed me how easily our culture justifies sexual aggression and trivializes the seriousness of sexual violence, ensuring its perpetuation.

It also didn't help that I live in a state where "liberal" is a dirty word. I remain politically independent, so I am not beholden to a party or leader's particular policy or agenda that does not align with my values. But I support liberal causes—social justice, women's equality, civil liberties, human rights, equal opportunity, abolition of systems that keep people down, and humanitarian efforts.

Ironically, I was not raised around liberal political values, nor was I "indoctrinated" in higher education. On the contrary, I attended a conservative university. My graduate studies, however, sparked my curiosity, leading me to delve into new fields of knowledge, and awakened the understanding that all human knowledge is connected. My travels opened a portal to societies, places, and cultures I never knew existed. In my studies and travels, I have learned critical thinking, evidence-based truth-seeking, and global awareness along with empathy, curiosity, and humility. I now view issues in the larger context of the world, not just my own experiences. I have become more aware of the suffering of others and feel a moral responsibility to address it. Therefore, in my current profession as an HR leader, I strive to make the office a safer and more equitable place, and I, likewise, want that for the world.

Hearing many of my friends and loved ones disparage people who share my values exacerbated my loneliness and reinforced the feeling I didn't belong where I was. My therapist, moreover, who had been my main pillar of support and had helped me so much, informed me she was to move out of state.

I felt utterly alone.

At work, I went into the Wellness Room to meditate. I reached inside myself, searching for something to hang on to, but I felt myself drifting away. I wondered not only how I was going to get through the day, but through the next hour.

CHAPTER 23
White Light

Oklahoma City
November 2016

OUT OF DESPERATION, I WENT to yoga class to see my teacher Dee. Since conventional methods weren't alleviating my depression, I asked her, a sixty-some-year-old hippy, if she would give me a Reiki treatment. At the end of yoga class, she placed her hands on my head and my heart. While I didn't feel instant relief, the treatment helped somewhat. I will be the first to admit no scientific evidence supports the effectiveness of Reiki. Yet, I have experienced remarkable outcomes from it, in particular, the release of powerful emotions that were "blocking" my chakras.

"Would you like to go with me to the Spirit Fair?" she asked. "I am going to see Lisette, the angel therapist."

I had seen the event on Facebook a few weeks before, but dismissed it as too "kooky." Albeit that day, I was receptive.

"Sure," I said. "I'll meet you over there."

As I drove to the Spirit Fair, tears flowed from my eyes. *Why won't this let up?*

When I arrived, a sea of booths featuring palm readings, tarot card interpretations, and energy healings spread the room, along with an array of perfumed oils, incense, herbs, statuaries, crystals, candles, and Himalayan salt lamps. As open-minded as I am, I felt foolish. *What am I doing here?*

Lisette, an attractive, middle-aged Puerto-Rican woman, knew nothing about me. She took both of my hands in hers, and I felt her warmth and compassion.

"We will start out with a prayer," she said, reciting the Our Father.

I repeated it with her, something I hadn't done in years. While I no longer practice Catholicism, I found comfort in the sounds and the familiarity of the prayer. Studying her table, I also noticed statues of the Virgin Mary and the Archangels Gabriel, Raphael, and Michael.

"You're Catholic," I said.

"Yes. Who do you want to hear from?" Lisette asked me.

"My dad and my grandma," I said without hesitation.

"Hmm . . . I am not getting a strong reading on your father," she said, "but I feel your grandmother powerfully." Lisette concentrated and said, "She is saying not to be so hard on yourself. She says to tell you her white light surrounds you."

I nearly fell out of my chair. *Grandma's white light! The same one she spoke of whenever I was afraid.*

Lisette added, "And your father is very proud of you and loves you. He wishes he had told you that more often when you were a little girl."

Again, tears rolled down my cheeks. Lisette did not know when my father died. For all she knew, it could have been the previous year.

"There's something else," she said. "You're heartbroken."

"Yes," I confirmed, dabbing my eyes. "My family doesn't understand me, and my therapist is moving away."

"Your family loves you," she said. "They just want you to be happy. And your therapist is one of many healers you will encounter along your path. You will always have a connection to her."

I contemplated what Lisette said.

"Is there anything else you want to ask?" she inquired.

"Will I always feel so alone?" I asked.

"You have trouble opening yourself up because you're afraid of being abandoned," she said.

She had no idea how right that was.

"You hold yourself back with negative affirmations," she continued. "You need to reprogram your mind with *positive* affirmations. Next year, you will go through a major transformation," she continued. "I see you traveling and writing. Everyone will look at you and wonder what happened to you—in a good way. You just have to face your fear."

She didn't know I was a traveler and a writer.

When I left Lisette, I felt wonderful. In that moment, the depression and anxiety lifted, and a ray of light pierced and suffused the darkness. For the first time, I became aware of birds chirping outside, celebrating the mild autumn day. As the weight of the last few weeks rose from my chest, I exhaled. I laughed as I thought about Grandma. Of course she would connect with me through a Catholic psychic!

I took great comfort in what Lisette told me. I would not only have a future, but a glorious one.

CHAPTER 24

Penumbra

Oklahoma City

November – December 2016

I STROLLED OUTSIDE TO A magnificent fall day. The late autumn sun shined on my face as I inhaled the fresh, balmy air. The sun tinged its golden light on the leaves, transforming to red, yellow, and orange.

Next, I felt her resting on my shoulder. She was all too familiar—slight and unassuming, present but not assertive. She seemed at ease, like a bird perched on a branch. I tried to brush her off as I climbed into my car.

She grew larger while I commuted to work. She was a little more pressing now. She wanted me to pay attention. I tried to focus elsewhere—on my best friends, the stunning view of the lake, a looming deadline at work. *If I do that, maybe she will go away.*

But as the minutes passed, she became more demanding. She was no longer sitting on my shoulder, but clinging to my back, waiting for me to acknowledge her presence. She seeped into my eyes, distorting my world to fit her dark-colored lens, and into my mind—so that my awareness was no longer in the present world, but on her.

But my senses were not enough. She was on a warpath. Why stop now?

My body came next. Her legs became my legs, and her arms became my arms. Small tasks became marathons. My movements were no longer one fluid act, but separate and robotic motions. I opened my mouth to speak, but couldn't think of what I wanted to say.

When I arrived at my office, I looked in the mirror, and my face—HoHo's face—was gone. The silent figure that once sat on my shoulder was staring back at me. We were one.

The portal of light that streamed over me the day before slammed shut without warning, a latch falling into place. She, the depression, enveloped me again. It was the monster I couldn't get away from.

Since I was thirteen, I had suffered through severe depression every November and December. Only now it was worse. My insurance, which paid for eighty percent of my mental health benefits, threatened to cut or eliminate my coverage—when I needed it the most. My therapist would try to plead my case.

In anguish, I called my mother.

"I can't get it to stop. It won't go away," I cried.

"Honey, I love you so much. It's going to be okay," she said. "Depression and anxiety run in our family. You'll get through this."

I tried to find comfort in what she said, reminding myself that was the only language she could comprehend. She thought I was suffering from depression, anxiety, and the effects of perimenopause, which I was—but she didn't want to acknowledge the context. She didn't want to recognize the PTSD, the sexual abuse, or the pain of her not accepting what happened. I couldn't verbalize the deep-seated loneliness I felt, the heartbreak of her not understanding me. I knew she loved me and was helping me as much as she could, but I needed her to concede what I was going through.

My therapist recommended I see a doctor, who could prescribe me antidepressant medication. I knew other people who used it, and I didn't object to it. Even so, I thought, *That's okay for other people, but not for me. The only way I'll take any medication is if I feel like jumping in front of a moving car—but I am not one of those people.*

It turned out I *am* one of those people.

"Honey, there is no shame," Mom told me. "Lots of people take it."

Medication was the only remedy I had not tried. Maybe my depression did have a medical component. I had tried all the non-medical treatments—exercising, eating well, getting enough sleep, reading self-help books, going to therapy. All those practices helped, but not enough to pull me from my well of despair. I called the doctor to schedule an appointment, but she couldn't see me until after Christmas, almost a month away. That seemed like an eternity. *How will I make it until then?*

In the meantime, Mom called me and said she had a picture to send me. "I found this at your uncle's house," she said. "I had never seen it before."

A minute later, I received a text message. It was a photo of Grandma holding me as a baby. My heart filled with love and reassurance. Grandma was still with me.

* * *

AFTER CHRISTMAS, I SAW A couple of doctors. First, I went to an OBGYN, who confirmed I had all the symptoms of perimenopause, including hot flashes, night sweats, and insomnia, which were affecting my sleep and moods. She prescribed me low-dosage estrogen to regulate my hormones.

Next, I visited the psychiatrist my therapist recommended. As I filled out the doctor's questionnaire, one question leapt out at me: Have you felt like you wanted to be dead recently? *Shit, do I have to tell someone else?* I already felt so exposed.

Thankfully, the doctor, who was about ten years younger and personable, helped put me at ease. She diagnosed me with PTSD and major depressive disorder.

"You are high-functioning," she said. "So, I am going to prescribe you a low dosage of Prozac. It's an oldie, but a goodie."

I, nevertheless, was leery about taking it. "Is it going to change my personality?" I asked. "Or make it where I don't feel emotions?"

"No," she explained. "It will just stabilize you. It may take about a month to take effect."

The first couple of days I took the medication, I felt sluggish. Worrying I would fall asleep at work, I switched to taking it at night and prayed it would help.

Part Five
TOUCHING THE SKY

CHAPTER 25

Learning to Fly

Oklahoma City
Spring 2017

I WATCHED JILL, A FACE I had known for twenty-four years, on Facebook Live. A former high school classmate and certified life coach, Jill was someone I knew but didn't really *know*. Interacting periodically in school, we ran in different crowds, and I didn't have the opportunity to befriend her. Even so, we had been "friends" on Facebook for several years, and I followed her life coach business page. After all these years, she was still stunning, with lustrous dark blonde hair, impeccable nails and makeup, and a mellifluous voice that immediately soothed anyone who listened to her.

In January 2017, Jill started a thirty-day Facebook Live challenge, where she went live every evening around nine o'clock. After receiving the notifications, I began to watch her. Speaking in her soft, reassuring voice, Jill coached women who had lost sense of who they are. She encouraged them to remember who they were before the world told them how they are supposed to live and act.

"The little girl inside us doesn't want us to feel pain or rejection, so she tells us we need to fit in," Jill said. "I am here to teach women how to reclaim themselves and live with more joy, purpose, and empowerment."

Listening to her every night uplifted me. The portal of light cracked open, widening its aperture and spilling its rays on my face. This time it did not close. Between Jill's videos and the medication, I felt something I hadn't felt in weeks: hope.

So much of what Jill taught resonated with me. In some ways, I was afraid to live as my authentic self because it differed from my family or my community's values. To be progressive, worldly, and broad-minded in Oklahoma was challenging and sometimes isolating. Jill asked her audience how they wanted to feel. I sure as heck didn't want to feel the way I had been feeling. In what was the most enlightening idea I had heard in a while, she invited her viewers to create the life they had always wanted to live.

I knew one thing for certain: I was tired of fitting in. As wonderful as most Okies and my family are, I wasn't here to conform with everyone around me. I was here to be me, and I knew I needed to start living my values more openly.

I found the perfect opportunity with the Women's March of 2017. Joining millions of people around the globe, I marched for women's rights and engaged in the largest peaceful demonstration in US history. It was one of the most galvanizing and empowering causes I had ever participated in!

Best of all, I began finding my people, the ones who understood my journey. Maybe I wasn't alone. Maybe I had been seeking a connection where it couldn't be found. I so much wanted my family to be my everything, to walk this road with me, but perhaps they couldn't.

After watching Jill for several nights on her live videos, I felt drawn to work with her. *Should I email her for a complimentary one-on-one call?*

A voice inside of me echoed, *She was one of the cool kids in high school. What would you have in common with her?* Of course, Jill would say that was my "inner mean girl" talking. Ultimately, I chose to message her.

She said she would love to speak with me! For our call, she gave me an assignment: She asked me to record my "victim" story in pencil and my "hero" story in ink. I knew my victim story well, so that wasn't difficult to recall. Writing my hero story, on the other hand, was something I hadn't done.

When we spoke, she asked me to read both stories aloud to her. I felt awkward. Here I was, sharing the most intimate details of my life with someone I recognized, but hardly knew. However, she opened my mind to a possibility I hadn't considered. Maybe I could be a hero—to myself. At the end of our conversation, she said I could work with her for three months, or if I didn't feel right about it, I had no obligation to her. Casting aside my insecurities, I decided to go for it.

* * *

FORTY-TWO, THE BIRTHDAY THAT marked I would live longer than my father. I wondered if he had deeds or dreams he wished he had fulfilled before he died so young. I knew one thing: There was still so much I wanted to do. I wanted to live a life of adventure, even if it meant living with some risk. I wanted to experience the Earth's wonders and immerse myself in its beauty, treasures, people, and culture. If I were going to die, it wouldn't be because of depression. I had to start living true to myself.

What better way to commence my new phase than to go

skydiving! It was daring, yet typically harmless, and was a new horizon I could reach. I could plunge literally and figuratively into my new life! Of course, I wouldn't tell my mother until after I did it. She would worry too much and try to talk me out of it.

I was originally going to dive on my actual birthday, but after viewing the weather forecast, I determined the day before would be ideal. The exceptionally warm winter day with crystal blue skies and wisps of clouds beckoned me.

My friend Jenny and I arrived at the skydiving center with the other crazies who had signed up.

"Are you sure you don't want to try it?" I taunted Jenny.

"No, I'm good. I'll just watch you," she said.

Our instructor Quinn, a striking man in his early thirties, introduced himself to us.

"Hey, everyone, this is going to be fun," he said. "I will tell you exactly what to do."

As he delved into a detailed description of how to attach the harness, how to position ourselves in the airplane, and how to jump, I thought, *Oh god, I hope I remember all this.* On top of that, I had to sign several pages of liability waivers acknowledging that skydiving is risky, and that I was putting my life on the line.

Quinn and the videographer helped strap me into my harness, with two straps going over my shoulders, one around my waist, and two around my legs.

When we approached the plane, I was ecstatic to see a Cessna, just like the plane my dad used to fly my family in! This type of plane was more compact than I remembered, accommodating only three passengers and the pilot. It was wide enough only to line up single file—the pilot, the videographer, me, and Quinn. The radio crackled to life, and the tower gave the pilot all-clear for takeoff. With a roar, the plane lifted off and coasted into the air.

As we took off, my anticipation mounted. Unlike flying in a commercial jet, I could feel the slightest undulations of the plane. Every thousand feet, Quinn announced our altitude: two thousand . . . three thousand . . . four thousand . . .

At four thousand feet, it already seemed like we were soaring, and we still had six thousand feet to go. As we ascended, the cabin became chilly, and I wasn't sure if my goose bumps stemmed from the frigid air or my heightening anxiety.

As we approached ten thousand feet, Quinn said, "Okay, let's move into position."

With barely enough room to rise, Quinn stood behind me and attached his harness to mine. He was the one with the parachute, so we needed to be secure.

"Okay, put on your goggles," he instructed.

Wrapping his arms around my waist, he yelled, "Door!"

Cold wind gusted into the plane. The videographer stepped out first and waited for us on the wing, so he could jump at the same time we did. Quinn nudged me toward the open door. I stared at my feet on the precipice, overlooking thousands of feet between me and the ground.

I can't believe I'm doing this. I hope I don't mess this up and knock my head on the wing. Or what if I collide with the videographer?

At that moment, I sensed my dad sitting on the wing and smiling.

"You got this, HoHo," he said. "I am here."

I looked down one last time at the world below me, a woven tapestry of abstract cities, fields, and forests.

"All right, we're ready," Quinn said. "Three, two, one . . . "

Before I knew it, Quinn pushed us out of the plane into the atmosphere.

The shock to my senses both overwhelmed and delighted me. The current rushed around me.

"Woooo! This is fuckin' awesome!" I yelled. Only a piece of silk spared me from possible death. This was the world as I had never experienced it. I was flying! For the first time in my life, nothing separated me from the earth but thousands of feet of open air.

As we plunged belly-down toward the earth, I waved my arms and smiled at the videographer only a few feet away from me, who was recording the whole experience.

Within thirty seconds, Quinn deployed the parachute, and the whirlwind diminished to a zephyr.

It was just me and the sky. Freedom. Bliss. An expanse of sweet calm.

As soon as the parachute unfurled, the air foisted us to a sitting position.

"Now is where you get to have fun with the parachute," Quinn said. He showed me how to execute 360-degree turns and how to change directions, gliding through the air.

Soon the ground came into focus.

"Okay, let's get ready for our landing. Keep your knees bent at a ninety-degree angle, and we will land on our feet," Quinn said.

"Hollie!" I heard Jenny screaming below.

"Jenny!" I yelled, as we closed in on the landing site. My feet hit the ground with a thud, where I ran a few steps until I could stop the momentum.

"Oh my god!" I screamed. "That's the most thrilling thing I've ever done!"

"You did it!" Jenny exclaimed and hugged me.

I was one day shy of forty-two, and I had been reborn.

* * *

I WAS HIGH AS A kite. No one could slap the smile off my face. The scariest part of the experience was calling my mom when I returned home.

"Mom, guess what I did?"

"What?" she asked.

"I went skydiving today!"

"You what?"

"I went skydiving. Don't worry. I'm in one piece," I told her. "It was the most exciting thing I have ever done!"

"What made you want to do that?"

"I wanted to do something bold to celebrate my birthday."

"Oh no! I am so glad I didn't know," she said.

"That's why I waited to tell you." I grinned. "You'll see the pictures on Facebook in a few minutes."

"I can't believe you did that," she said.

Between the afterglow of the dive and the medication taking effect, I was feeling much better. I continued to meet weekly with my therapist through videoconferencing and with Jill through phone sessions. In one session with my therapist, I described a dream I had in which I was the outsider viewing the assault, almost like watching a movie. Unlike my previous dreams, I didn't feel the terror of reliving the experience.

"That's a major breakthrough," my therapist said. "Instead of reliving the event like it's happening to you right now, you are observing it and standing outside of it. Your brain is time-stamping the event as occurring in the past, rather than the present."

Wow! The treatments were working. My brain was healing.

Even though I had been victimized, I didn't want to claim the title "victim" for myself. And I no longer wanted to be just a "survivor." I wanted to transcend what had happened to me, to lead a life of openness and wonder. To do that, I realized the coping strategies I had adopted to survive had worked well for a time, but were no longer serving me. They weren't propelling me forward on my healing journey.

Almost my entire life, I wondered who I would be if I hadn't been assaulted or my dad hadn't died. Jill taught me to see my true essence—who I am no matter what happens to me. I will never forget the day she said to me, "Hollie, you are *not* the assault." Her statement hit me like a lightning bolt. The assault had been my identity—but no more. Through our work together, Jill helped me rediscover who I am. Of course, I had to remember who I was before the boys assaulted me. I was HoHo—the name I had given myself as a child—a free spirit, both silly and serious, thoughtful and intellectually curious, who dreamed of one day exploring exotic locations and embarking on unique adventures, much like the ones I encountered in the Choose Your Own Adventure and science fiction novels I used to read. More than anything, I yearned to travel and learn about other people and cultures from different times and places.

It was as if I was meeting parts of myself for the first time in decades, and I was forty-two years old. I discovered that through all the traumas and losses, I had never really lost myself.

"You're still HoHo," Jill said. "You always have been."

So, I unlocked and unleashed her—I set my wild, adventurous self free. With that, I took another plunge to fulfill one of my greatest dreams—climbing Mount Kilimanjaro.

CHAPTER 26

Leveling Up

Oklahoma City
Summer 2017

SO MUCH OF WHAT I had done in my life was the result of someone else's influence or preferences. I wanted to show everyone—most of all myself—that I was making my life completely my own. To me, Kilimanjaro represented more than a mountain to conquer: It was the embodiment of all I thought had been out of reach. Better yet, I planned my trip to coincide with the Mount Kilimanjaro Marathon in June 2017, which I would run while I was in Africa.

My childhood fascination with Africa cast a permanent spell on me. Stories like "Ali Baba and the Forty Thieves" first drew me to Morocco eight years prior. Indeed, one of the most enchanting experiences of my life was when I trekked through the majestic dunes of the Sahara Desert. I gazed out at the ocean of orange swells, each dune's crest shaped into a sharp edge by the wind, as I beheld the sun casting its shadows on the crimson sand. I was living in another place and time, in the ancient folktales of *The Arabian Nights*. I basked in the soothing serenity on the peak of a colossal dune until the sun receded into a faint reddish glow over the horizon.

This time, I was going to sub-Saharan Africa, the captivating world of lions, zebras, giraffes, acacia trees, and, of course, Kilimanjaro. Rising from the plains of Moshi to an astounding 19,341 feet at its summit, Kilimanjaro is the tallest freestanding mountain in the world. One must trudge through five different ecosystems and multiple microclimates to climb it. Never mind I had never gone backpacking before or scaled any mountain above twelve thousand feet. *I am an endurance athlete. Climbing Kilimanjaro couldn't be harder than running a marathon or ultramarathon.*

Nonetheless, the prospect of climbing the mountain *and* running a marathon back-to-back daunted me. I had confidence in my physical ability to climb Kilimanjaro and certainly in my desire. *But to run a full marathon afterward?* Completing a marathon in itself is grueling, and I had no idea what my physical shape would be after conquering one of the seven summits. With reluctance, I decided to attempt the climb and run the half marathon. That would still be an honorable achievement.

* * *

SINCE I DIDN'T HAVE THE fortune of training in high altitude, I had to simulate conditions as closely as possible in Oklahoma. Mostly, I ran around my neighborhood in a black oxygen deprivation mask that made me look like Kylo Ren from *Star Wars*, or, worse yet, the eccentric neighborhood lady, which is probably how I am known, anyway. By adjusting the flux valves on the mask, I could control the airflow. Even on the low setting, though, I felt like I was suffocating when I ran. I would have to stop after a few meters, gasping for air.

Surely the altitude would not be that stifling.

Consequently, I didn't use the mask much, believing if I primed myself in other ways, I would be adequately prepared. I ran up to twelve miles in my training runs and lifted weights regularly. Coupled with my new vegetarian diet, I was the slimmest and leanest I had been in years.

* * *

A FEW DAYS BEFORE I was to leave, Bob, who had been diagnosed with cancer about ten years earlier, took a turn for the worse. He was now under hospice care. Usually elegantly dressed, Bob, instead, donned a medical gown. Withered to a portion of his former self, he was barely conscious. Somehow, I knew he was close to the end of his earthly existence. I teared up as I thought about my dad and John. I never got to say goodbye to them. Now the Universe was giving me an opportunity I had never had. I would get to say goodbye to Bob.

"I love you like a father," I told him.

"Why are you telling me this?" he mumbled.

"Because it's true. You've been so good to me. Thank you for making my mom so happy the last ten years," I said, wiping away the tears.

"I love you too," he said.

I sat with him and held his hand for several minutes, knowing it would be the last time I saw him. I took one final look at him, my face red and swollen, and said, "Watch me when I'm on Kilimanjaro," and squeezed his hand. He passed away the next day.

* * *

WITH MY UPCOMING TRIP, I had no time to process Bob's death. I was going to be absent from work for three weeks, and I had to make sure I briefed my colleagues on the responsibilities they needed to cover while I was away, not to mention pack for the journey. Subsequently, I didn't end up leaving work until eight thirty p.m. on my last day. I had promised my seventeen-year-old nephew Jack I would take him out to dinner before I left. At first, I thought maybe he wanted his birthday present early. After all, the boy *loves* his birthday. To my surprise, he didn't bring it up once.

Even sitting down, his long, slender frame towered over me. He said, "I'm not going to see you for three weeks. I'll miss you."

What a sweet boy! He could always charm me with his baby blue eyes and winsome smile.

"I'll miss you too," I said.

"How high is Mount Kilimanjaro?" he asked me.

"19,341 feet," I replied.

"There's not a chance you could die, could you?" he asked.

"Oh, no, sweetie, I am not going to die," I told him. "It's going to be fun."

Poor boy! I don't know if he was a little worried because Bob had just passed away. Maybe that was one reason he wanted to see me. I, too, was heavyhearted about Bob's passing. I was going to miss his funeral the day I flew out and thought about postponing my trip to support my mom.

But Mom said, "Bob was so excited for you. He would want you to go."

When I returned home, I spent almost the entire night packing, but it was totally worth it to see my boy. Unlike previous trips, I had so many things to consider. I had never gone on such an extensive excursion before. I not only had to remember normal everyday clothes and items but also all the specialty gear for climbing Kilimanjaro. I needed to pack for all types of weather—hot, windy, freezing, and wet. The minimalist in me said to pack only the bare necessities, not the contingent items. At the same time, I didn't know what I would need and how accessible the items would be in Tanzania. In fact, I almost didn't pack my rain gear. Then I imagined myself slogging through viscous, knee-deep mud in the dense rainforest on Kilimanjaro and reconsidered. That was not a situation I wanted to be in.

After packing and repacking, double and triple-checking my list, and second-guessing myself, I ended up with one sizable twenty-eight-inch suitcase, a ninety-liter duffel bag, and my backpack. I would have to check the two larger bags with the airline, but I determined it was better to bring too much, rather than too little.

The adventure I had planned months for was about to begin.

CHAPTER 27
Down in Africa

Africa
June 2017

I SLEPT ONLY ABOUT ONE hour before my alarm jolted me awake. I was both excited and exhausted. The endless preparation and training over the last few months culminated to this moment. There was nothing more I could do. Everything I had done would have to suffice. Despite the lack of sleep, I knew I could snooze on my flight, even though I don't typically nap well on planes. At least I would get to check into a hotel in Washington, DC, and not have to fly to Africa until the following morning.

When I arrived at Dulles, I had to get a Smart Cart to haul all my luggage. The shuttle driver looked at me like, "How can one lady pack so much crap?" *For real*, I agreed with him. If it weren't for the athletic bags, he might have taken me for a fussy, high-maintenance woman who packs her entire closet.

When I arrived at the ticket counter to check in, the line was about one hundred people deep and lagged almost to a standstill. I started timing how long the ticket agents spent on each customer. I thought I had arrived in plenty of time for my flight, but at this rate,

I didn't know and started getting nervous. Moreover, since it was a non-US airline, my TSA pre-check privileges would do no good.

To my relief, about fifteen minutes later, a man at the platinum ticket counter motioned me over.

"I will save you some time," he said in his Ethiopian-English accent.

I am not sure how I got chosen for this privilege, but I welcomed it.

* * *

I ARRIVED AT MY GATE and saw a classy senior woman, reminiscent of a Classic Hollywood actress. That had to be Marie, the race director for the trip.

She walked over, smiled, and said, "You must be Hollie."

I grinned and shook her hand. "You must be Marie."

She hugged me and kissed me on the cheek. "I could tell it was you because you look like a runner," she said.

I could look like worse things.

"The line was really long," I told her. "Luckily, I got singled out to go to platinum."

"He must have known you are a runner," Marie said.

I wasn't sure how that gave me priority.

"Everyone moves slowly in Africa," she continued. "They take their time and don't get upset if something goes wrong because something usually does go wrong."

She turned and said, "Let me introduce you to Jimmy. He is part of our group, and he is going to climb the mountain. He is seventy-five."

"Great to meet you, Jimmy," I said, shaking his slender hand.

"I can't wait to tell my mom someone her age is climbing with me!"

I grinned at his thin, white-bearded face, but by his expression, I wasn't sure if he liked my comment. Nonetheless, I thought he was amazing. *I have no excuses not to make it*, I thought.

An hour later, we boarded our flight to Addis Ababa, Ethiopia. Having never been to Ethiopia, my only image was that of starving children enduring blinding dust and overpowering heat. Of course, my mind thought back to the drought of the early '80s and the ensuing USA for Africa campaign, beautifully commemorated in the song "We Are the World." I was curious to see what Ethiopia looked like in person.

* * *

IN THE INTERLUDES BETWEEN READING books and watching movies, I stared at the flight path screen as the plane cruised over land and sea, across the Atlantic, and through Libya, Egypt, and Sudan. For several restless hours, I watched the ground below transition from brown scrub and bronze desert into a deep escarpment revealing the lush, mountainous plateau of Ethiopia.

Despite pictures I had seen in *National Geographic*, I was unprepared for what I would see as the plane slipped into and out of the thin, scattered haze over Addis Ababa. Dense forests of eucalyptus trees and verdant hillsides encircled a sprawling metropolis of bustling boulevards, tightly packed one- and two-story buildings, and ubiquitous skyscrapers. This former mountain empire was nothing like I imagined, nor like the Ethiopia that had been portrayed to me. Consequently, I felt like one of those unenlightened people who think Oklahoma is all cowboys and Indians.

Addis Ababa is also the third highest capital in the world,

sitting eight thousand feet above sea level in the Entoto Mountains. *This would be a great training ground for Kilimanjaro.* Viewing it from above, I wished I could stay longer and visit the city.

* * *

WHEN WE LANDED, IT WAS a relief to get off the plane. I got to meet the other people in our group, among them Mary and Charlie, an attractive marathon supercouple older than me, who lived in Georgia. Even though the airport was modern and bustling, we had no internet connection. So much for letting my mom know I arrived safely.

A few hours later, we boarded our plane to Arusha, Tanzania. We had only to fly over the southern half of Ethiopia and the expanse of Kenya to get to Tanzania. It might seem like it would be a short flight, but because Africa is so enormous, it took hours. As we traveled deeper into Kenya, the greenery gave way to a barren, mountainous amber landscape, similar to images I had seen of the surface of Mars. That was one thing I loved about Africa, even on my previous visits. I felt like I was entering another world.

As the hours lagged on, I peered out the window and saw Kilimanjaro—regal but unassuming, rising above the thick blanket of silky clouds. I imagined myself standing on her fabled peak. Most of her outline was cloaked from view, like an iceberg veiled in the cerulean depths of the ocean.

She looked just like she did in pictures, except even grander and more majestic. To think I would be standing on her peak in just a few days—on a glacier in equatorial Africa—seemed surreal. In essence, climbing Kilimanjaro from base to summit is like traveling from the equator to Antarctica. I would traverse five distinct ecological zones—the emerald greenery of the rainforest; the rugged, rocky trails of the heather and moorland; the sparsely vegetated low alpine; and the piercing winds of the arctic desert.

While no one knows the precise origin of the word "Kilimanjaro," it is widely believed to derive from the Swahili word *Kilima,* meaning "mountain," and the KiChagga word *Njaro,* loosely translated as "whiteness." *Mountain of whiteness. I like that.* Another theory is that "Kilimanjaro" is the European pronunciation of a KiChagga phrase meaning "we failed to climb it." I naturally preferred the first interpretation.

Of course, Kilimanjaro is not a mountain in the traditional sense, but a stratovolcano, formed by layers of lava, cinder, and ash that have accumulated through its eruptive phases. It soars over nineteen thousand feet above sea level with a base that sprawls forty miles across the surrounding plains. Overall, Kilimanjaro encompasses a colossal fifteen hundred square miles.

Comprised of three prominent peaks, Kilimanjaro represents three eras of volcanic activity from the last one million years—Mawenzi in the east, Shira in the west, and Kibo in the center. Mawenzi and Shira have largely eroded over the millennia, but Kibo, the youngest of the peaks and the one we were going to climb, retains its volcanic shape with a caldera spanning over a mile.

While Shira and Mawenzi are now extinct—meaning they are unlikely to erupt again—Kibo, the highest peak, is merely dormant, signifying it shows no signs of volcanic unrest. Nonetheless, scientists expect it to become active in the indeterminate future. Although they estimate the last major eruption occurred about 360,000 years ago, they recorded volcanic activity only two hundred years ago. I was taking my chances it wouldn't erupt.

* * *

WHEN WE ARRIVED AT KILIMANJARO International Airport, Tanzania welcomed us with lavish flora, towering palm trees, and jovial faces. As soon as we disembarked, I changed into capri pants, athletic sandals, and a wide-rimmed blue safari hat. I was happy to see that everyone else packed as much stuff as I did.

A shuttle took us from Arusha to our hotel in Moshi, the town closest to the main routes going up Kilimanjaro. Canary-yellow flowers, shamrock-green shrubs, and tall, arching trees lined the walkways on the hotel grounds, no doubt luxurious compared to the surrounding area. My room was small, simple, and neat with two firm twin beds. Diaphanous white netting hung over the beds, and I wondered what purpose it served. I soon found out. I had to sleep with netting over my entire bed, or I would get devoured by mosquitos. That is not such a grave concern in the US. By contrast, malaria-carrying mosquitos pervade certain parts of Tanzania, and it is best not to get bitten in the first place. With the country so close to the equator, the tropical climate attracts all kinds of critters.

After twenty-four hours of traveling, I thought it would be refreshing to take a shower. As I turned on the faucet, ice-cold water streamed out, taking several minutes to warm up to a lukewarm temperature. I surveyed the floor and saw a trail of ants scaling the wall. Oh well, if they didn't bother me, I wouldn't bother them. One night of relative luxury before we hit the trails!

That evening we had dinner at the hotel, where Rutta, our affable head guide, briefed us on tomorrow's climb. In his forties, I wondered how he maintained his burnished dark skin and bright smile after dozens of ascents up Kilimanjaro. Likewise, I met others who would become my good friends over the course of the excursion—Saint and Chris, two fit, good-looking young men from Singapore; Shawn, an avid marathoner and Spartan runner from upstate New York; and Mark from Virginia, who had climbed to Everest Base Camp—plus Charlie, Mary, and Jimmy, whom I had already met.

Charlie lifted his white cap off his ash-colored hair and put it back on. "Which one are you running—the full or the half?" he asked in his charming Southern accent.

"The half," I answered. "If we were running the marathon before the climb, I would run the full. I just don't know how I will be physically after the climb."

"Do the full," Charlie said. "That way you can get another continent."

Mary leaned forward and pushed a lock of her blonde hair behind her ear. "Yes," she said. "I'm running the full. You can do it with me."

"I haven't trained for a full marathon," I told them. "The longest I have run recently is twelve miles."

"You can do it if you take it slowly," Charlie said. "I'll tell you how to do it."

There's nothing like the bad influence of other runners to talk me into crazy exploits. Charlie, who was in his sixties, had run over one hundred marathons. By the time we had finished our conversation, I asked Marie about running the full.

"No other woman is signed up for the half," she told me. "You would be guaranteed to win it."

Nonetheless, I thought of my deep desire to run a *full* marathon on all seven continents. When was the next time I would be here?

That night, I laid my tank top, shorts, hat, sunglasses, hiking boots, trekking poles, and hydration pack on the adjacent bed. The moment I had dreamed about for so long was here. I felt energized and self-assured, about to embark on the journey of my life.

CHAPTER 28

Monkeys in the Mist

Mount Kilimanjaro
June 18, 2017 – Day 1

THE NEXT MORNING, I AWOKE to absolute calm, peering out my back balcony as the dawn broke. The black curtain of the night sky began to fade and evolve into embers of orange and gold. As the sky illuminated, I bolted upright at what I saw—Mount Kilimanjaro! The clouds the day before had completely obscured it. I dressed in my outdoor gear, pulling on my shorts and boots, so I could sit on my balcony and marvel at her. For a moment, it was just the mountain and me. I reveled in the stillness of the crisp air and freshness of the morning dew, enjoying the last few minutes of solitude before commencing on my odyssey.

After consuming a nourishing breakfast of fried eggs, toast, and fruit, my group and I climbed into our shuttle van and headed forty-five minutes away to the entrance of the Marangu route, the path we would navigate up Mount Kilimanjaro.

Out of the seven established paths to the summit, Marangu is regarded as the "easiest," jokingly called the "tourist route" or the "Coca-Cola route." But that is not why I chose it. Marangu is also the quickest, therefore the least expensive passage, taking only six days to complete. Between climbing Kilimanjaro, running the marathon, going on safari, and visiting Zanzibar, I was already going to be absent from work for three weeks. I didn't want to burden my colleagues any longer than I had to.

An hour's drive brought us to the end of the asphalt road, where it gave way to dust, bumps, and potholes. As we neared the entrance to Kilimanjaro National Park, the narrow, rutted roads took us through the village of Marangu, where I noticed a sign for a casket business.

"Oh, wow," I pointed out to my new friends, "at least they're prepared if we don't make it down." Bad joke, I know, but we all laughed.

At one point, our van stopped, and I observed a man leading a goat on a leash to another man riding a motorcycle. Motorcycle Man handed Goat Man some money, and Goat Man handed over the goat. Motorcycle Man's passenger scooped up the goat, cradling it like a baby, and hopped on the back of the motorcycle as it sped off. I was both fascinated and horrified by the transaction.

"That goat is not long for this world," I remarked.

* * *

THE MARANGU GATE LIES IN the thick of the rainforest at 6,195 feet. I had never been to a rainforest before, and I found the damp, chilly air and the neighboring veil of trees refreshing and invigorating. Even though we had just had breakfast, the guides fed us a calorie-dense lunch of sandwiches, mangos, avocados, and hard-boiled eggs. It was only about five miles to our first camp at Mandara Hut, but I figured I might as well eat again since I would need the fuel.

Everyone else in my group wore neutral or beige hiking pants and long-sleeve shirts, whereas I donned neon yellow running shorts, a royal blue tank top, and an electric blue sports hat.

"You're definitely the most colorful one here," Charlie told me. "Are you sure you're dressed warm enough?"

"Oh, yeah!" I said, smiling. "My hot flashes keep me warm."

I was actually somewhat chilled, but figured I would warm up once we began moving.

When I envisioned the start of our journey, I imagined bounding across the threshold of the trail and posting a photo to Facebook. The location is so remote, however, none of us had cell phone reception. Alas, the world would have to wait to see, and my mom would have to trust that I was okay.

Our adventure started out tantalizingly easy, as we made our way through the verdant canopy of ferns, sycamores, and junipers. On the dank, earthy forest floor, a cool stream trickled down the trail, meandering around jutting stones and roots. A few rays of golden sunlight pierced the canopy, creating a lace-patterned contrast of light and dark throughout the forest's magical understory of uninterrupted greenery. I was so absorbed by my surroundings that I stopped to take a photo every few seconds.

A soothing mist kissed the treetops and added an air of mystery. Thick coats of soft green moss covered the tree trunks, and the smell of fresh dew permeated the air. Among the dense tangle of branches, long, serpentine vines cascaded down, creating links between the trees. As we shuffled past, I overheard disturbances in the leaves. Stopping and spinning around, I discerned a family of adorable blue monkeys perched on the limbs, springing from tree to tree, gazing at me as I greeted them and took their photos.

Rutta said, "There are no restrooms before we reach Mandera Hut, so if you need to go, say you need to 'catch the monkey,' and we will know to stop."

Sure enough, at one point, someone had to run off into the trees and "catch the monkey." We figured if one of us had to catch the monkey, we might as well all go.

First mark of civilization gone.

With each step, we gained elevation, and my breath became shallow. The path was not technically challenging, but I had to remember we started at 6,200 feet and continued to ascend. Even though we were immersed in a tropical climate, we might as well have been hiking in the Rockies. The guides warned us to go "*pole, pole*," which means "slowly" in Swahili. We were losing oxygen the higher we advanced, and my daypack began to strain my shoulders. Water was my heaviest commodity, but I could not go without it. I had also packed all my rain gear, in case we got caught in a downpour. I had read stories about trekkers laboring for hours in the rain and wanted to be prepared.

After ambling for three hours through the dancing, filtered light of the forest, we emerged in a wide clearing under a brilliant cobalt sky. It was Mandara Hut, our first camp. Nestled in the wilderness, the camp included six tiny A-frame cabins with sleek green roofs, an outhouse, and a mess hall. To celebrate our venture up to nine thousand feet, our eighteen guides gathered around us and performed an enthusiastic a capella version of the "Song of Kilimanjaro," the obligatory tune taught to all climbers.

Jambo! Jambo, bwana!
Hello! Hello, sir!

Habari gani? Mzuri sana!
How are you? Very well!

Wageni, mwakaribishwa!
Guests, you are welcome!

Kilimanjaro? Hakuna matata!
Kilimanjaro? No trouble!

Tembea pole, pole. Hakuna matata!
Walk slowly, slowly. No trouble!

Utafika salama. Hakuna matata!
You'll get there safe. No trouble!

Kunywa maji mengi. Hakuna matata!
Drink plenty of water. No trouble!

Kilimanjaro, Kilimanjaro,
Kilimanjaro, Kilimanjaro,

Kilimanjaro, mlima mrefu sana.
Kilimanjaro, such a high mountain.

Na Mawenzi, na Mawenzi,
Also, Mawenzi, also, Mawenzi!

Na Mawenzi, mlima mrefu sana.
Also, Mawenzi, such a high mountain.

Ewe nyoka, ewe nyoka!
Like a snake, like a snake!

Ewe nyoka, mbona waninzunguka.
Like a snake, you wrap around me.

Wanizunguka, wanizunguka.
You wrap around me, you wrap around me.

Wanizunguka wataka kukila nyama.
Trying to eat me like a piece of meat.

Hakuna matata! That's a Swahili phrase most people know, thanks to *The Lion King*.

* * *

BECAUSE TANZANIA IS SO CLOSE to the equator, the sun rises around six thirty a.m. and sets at six thirty p.m. nearly the entire year. In the escalating chill of dusk, my friends and I met at the mess hall, where the chefs served us popcorn and steaming cups of tea and coffee. For dinner, they prepared us pepper steak, fried potatoes, roasted green beans, and hot cucumber soup. It appeared we would not go hungry.

As Mary and Charlie, my roommates, settled into our cabin, I wandered outside to view the wondrous night sky in the open dome over the surrounding forest. I gazed up at the stars, glistening like diamonds on black velvet, and watched the hazy band of the Milky Way move across the sky in a lazy arc. Seldom had I seen so many stars and never in the southern hemisphere. A shooting star grazed the edge of my vision, and I made a silent wish for a safe, successful passage.

When I returned to my cabin, I tried to sleep, but I was shaking with cold, even in my zero-degree sleeping bag. I had no idea what the temperature was, and I couldn't get my feet and hands to warm up. While the altitude had not bothered me so far, I took a Diamox to prevent altitude sickness. After some time, I lapsed into a shallow, fitful sleep a few hours before the guides woke us up.

CHAPTER 29
Africa's Giants

Mount Kilimanjaro
June 19, 2017 – Day 2

I AWOKE BEFORE DAYBREAK TO the guides rapping on our door. They had to rouse us early, so they could boil water from nearby streams and fill our hydration packs. They also left bowls of steaming hot water with fresh towels, so we could clean up and brush our teeth. Mary took off her glasses and wiped her face. I dunked the towel in the water and laid it over my head. The warm water felt so good on my icy hands and face. The camp had outdoor showers, but the water was so cold, it was unbearable. My friends and I opted to "freshen up" as best as we could with the hot water and towels.

Second mark of civilization gone.

As we packed, I wrestled with my sleeping bag to compress it in a tiny pouch, only about a third of its size. *It's too damn early for this.* After several unsuccessful attempts, Mary bundled it for me. I would have to get better at that.

We picked up the trail, the morning air swathed in mist, and I inhaled the fresh scent of the foliage. As we left the rainforest behind, the tall, majestic trees dwindled to a few scraggly, wind-gnarled bushes and evergreens. The sun broke over the tree line, revealing assorted shrubs, grasses, and lichen. We had entered the heather ecosystem, an expanse much sparser and drier than the rainforest. Of course, I was sporting my shorts and tank top from the day before, knowing I would warm up in no time. Sure enough, with only wild grasses, low-lying heather, and minimal tree cover, the temperature shot up.

Notwithstanding, I thought it would be an easy day. We had only seven miles to trek before reaching Horombo, our next camp. Even so, the ease of the previous day's hike lulled me into a false sense of security. The insidious, unconscious onset of brain fog from the rising altitude hindered my ability to convert meters to feet and to sense how high I was ascending.

At midday, the heather transitioned into moorland. Tussock grass, senecios, and lobelias now dominated the sprawling landscape. The dancing clusters of giant senecios welcomed us with their thick, shaggy arms of dry leaf buds and rosette crowns of spiky green leaves and bright lemon flowers. Without the refuge of the rainforest, the sun scorched us unpityingly. I had to keep guzzling water and dousing myself with sunblock.

The tundra-like terrain soon gave way to fields of rock and scree, as the path became less defined and more rugged and steep. Even with the aid of my trekking poles, loose stones slid under my feet, nearly making me roll an ankle. My boots started chafing my shins, as I struggled to maintain my balance on the unwieldy, shifting surface. My knees smarted from negotiating the jagged, grueling terrain, forcing me to fall back. My breathing grew more labored, as my daypack became progressively onerous. *Now I know what a horse feels like.* I tried to pack a lighter load than the day before, but the water still weighed me down. For the first time on our excursion, I muttered a string of expletives. I heard Mary, a few feet away from me, drop an F-bomb.

"Sorry," she said, chuckling.

I laughed and said, "Oh, I'm just getting started."

"Charlie hates that word," Mary whispered.

Such a Southern gentleman.

"You can say it all you want in front of me. If I'm not cussing, I'm not getting challenged enough," I explained.

To top it off, the higher elevation makes one increasingly bloated. I was grateful I brought some Tums. A couple of my new friends burped apologetically to get some relief.

I said, "If you have to let it loose, just do it. We're out in the middle of nowhere. We don't need to be so polite."

From then on, we just let it out.

Third mark of civilization gone.

By this time, we were learning each other's pace and falling into a comfortable cadence. As we traded stories about our mishaps and adventures, I realized this was my tribe. One of the most enthralling parts of these trips is not just the climbing, but the opportunities to get to know interesting people. Everyone has a fascinating story to tell about what they are doing and why they are doing it.

Despite the physical demands, I reveled in the surrealistic scenery. Surpassing the cloud line, we got a pristine view of the stunning ice-blue sky and the glacial peak of Kilimanjaro on the horizon. We stopped and rested on some boulders to eat our lunch, as gusts of wind swayed the occasional tufts of grass over the rocky plateau.

"We're just a couple of days away," said Rutta, pointing to the summit.

It was odd to think the summit we could see so clearly would take us a couple of days to reach.

After seven hours of navigating extensive tracts of rock debris, we made it to Horombo Hut at 12,200 feet. The day's colors dissolved into gray, and the senecios we left behind became opaque silhouettes of crouching giants. In the dying wind and pale yellow light of the sunset, I stood on the edge of the promontory at the end of the camp, looking out on the ocean of clouds, the sun casting its final rays on the billows of silver and bluish gray. Heaven and Earth seemed to flow seamlessly into each other, and I yearned to step out onto the undulating sea of white.

Meanwhile, the plunging temperature roused me out of my reverie. I was still wearing running shorts and a tank top and needed to put on more layers. Instead, I strode over to the mess hall, where the cooks served us popcorn, hot chocolate, and tea, like they did the day before. Despite the warm beverages, I was still freezing. Here on the edge of the alpine desert, temperatures could rise to one hundred degrees during the day and plummet below thirty-two degrees during the night. Grimacing in pain from my achy knees, I hobbled to the cabin to put on my pants and coat.

Once I arrived there, I really had to go to the lavatory. I could either stumble one hundred feet uphill over giant, obstructive rocks to the camp washroom or go just outside the camp right by my cabin. I opted to go out in the wild.

As soon as I began walking back to camp, one of the park rangers, wielding a massive gun, startled me.

"What are you doing?" he asked.

"Do you really want to know?" I asked him.

He just stared at me.

"I had to catch the monkey," I explained.

Never mind there were no monkeys anywhere near this altitude.

"Why didn't you go to the toilet?" he asked.

Toilet was a loose description for what they had. More like a hole in the ground.

"It's too far away, and my knees are killing me," I told him.

"You can't go in the park. You have to use the facility," he said.

Too late for that. I didn't see what the issue was. We didn't have a "facility" available for most of the excursion and usually had to use Mother Nature.

"Why didn't you use the facility?" he asked again.

"This conversation is making me uncomfortable," I told him. "I already told you why. I am going to dinner now."

As soon as I arrived at the mess hall, I told Rutta what had happened. He said, "Yeah, you can get fined. Which ranger was it?"

"I have no clue," I told him. "It just caught me off guard."

"Don't worry about it," Rutta said.

Filthy and sweaty, we sat down to dinner. Unlike the night before, the mess hall had no electricity, only the dim glow of candlelight. Every time the door opened, a new draught of wind grazed us, fluttering the flames. Still, my new friends and I laughed heartily, the warm glimmer of the fire shimmering off our cheeks, as we cradled the steaming cups of tea and hot chocolate.

Oddly enough, I wasn't hungry. Although I had read that high altitude could induce loss of appetite, I didn't feel sick. In any case, I made myself eat.

I roomed with Mary and Charlie again. Of course, we had the only cabin with no electricity. Oh well, we were just going to sleep there. We kept a flashlight by the door and devised a clever plan to elude the Potty Patrol.

"Turn off the flashlight when you get to the brush," I whispered to Charlie and Mary, "so they don't catch you, and I will be your lookout."

Charlie exited the cabin, peeked around, and slipped off into the darkness. He returned a few minutes later, having evaded detection. Mary and I followed suit. We were so proud of ourselves!

Settled in, I worried about my knees. I flopped onto my bed, wincing in agony, and lay there moaning. *Have I traveled ten thousand miles away from home and trained for four months just to have my knees give out on me? Hell no!* I would be damned if I were going to let my knees prevent me from reaching the summit. I needed ibuprofen badly, but I had already depleted my supply. Fortunately, Mary had some, so I took four tablets, along with some Diamox.

With deep fatigue and aching joints setting in, I collapsed into bed fully clothed and tried to sleep. Even wearing a fleece down coat, socks, and pants in my all-season sleeping bag, I couldn't warm up. After putting on gloves and shielding my face, I finally fell asleep.

CHAPTER 30

Arctic Desert

Mount Kilimanjaro
June 20, 2017 – Day 3

MY KNEES FELT SLIGHTLY BETTER when I woke up in the morning. As an extra precaution, I took three more ibuprofen. Meanwhile, my body was metamorphosing. Size-four hiking pants drooped on me, and I could tell I was getting thinner and leaner. Thankfully, after eating breakfast, the joint and muscle aches began to subside.

As we traversed the low alpine, the chill burned off rapidly, and I shed one layer of clothing. The morning sun painted the sky pink and orange, and Kilimanjaro seemed to beckon us in the distance.

The scenic morning stroll was fleeting, however. We now faced the longest, sharpest incline of our trek so far. It was even higher and tougher than the hill your grandmother climbed to go to school.

"This hill is a bitch," I muttered.

Like the day before, we had to maneuver around rocks and brush, except we were gasping for air two thousand feet higher. In some areas, I had to focus on my foot placement. My feet tried to find a flat place to land, but I usually had to let my heel strike a crevice in the stones before taking my next step. Of course, my knees didn't like this at all. I couldn't say whether I saw any vegetation or wildlife, unless one considered my group wildlife. By our bedraggled appearance, we *could* pass for wild animals. We plowed on, only one interminable, serpentine slope . . .

After what seemed like hours, we reached the crest, where we paused to take a breather. The porters traveled to a nearby stream and filled jugs of water to boil and drink.

We came upon a second hill and had to do it all over again.

"Bitch Hill Two," Charlie said.

Of course, the inclines may loom larger in my mind than they actually were, but we were also tackling harsh terrain two and a half miles above sea level, and we had been at it for three days.

After finishing the second rise, we came upon a boulder with markings that read *13,500*, referring to the elevation. We also spied a yellow and blue encirclement a few hundred yards from the trail.

"Is that where the aliens land?" I asked Rutta.

"No," he said, laughing. "That is where a helicopter can land, in case someone has to be medevacked to Nairobi."

Nairobi, Kenya, is a two-hour flight from anywhere on Mount Kilimanjaro. Now, Tanzania has its own search and rescue helicopters operating from nearby Moshi.

During our break, I fully absorbed my surroundings. Daisy-like yellow flowers called everlastings were scattered in the vast fields of ash-colored volcanic rock and pale green scraggly shrubs. I wondered how something as cheerful as an everlasting could survive at this altitude. After all, plant life here must survive the harsh conditions of drought, oppressive sun, and sub-zero temperatures—often in the same day.

It turns out the everlasting is the highest flowering plant on the mountain and can survive elevations up to fifteen thousand feet. The plants may look lovely, but they are no wilting lilies. Their stiff, dry structure helps them survive the scant moisture and frosty nights of the alpine desert, and their overlapping petals close at night, further protecting them against cold and water loss. I hope I am as tough as an everlasting!

The most riveting spectacle of all was Kilimanjaro itself. We were finally close enough to the Kibo cone to behold its impressive glaciers cast against the sparkling blue sky, clinging to the peak's steep ledges. This is the iconic view of Kilimanjaro, the one everyone comes to see. I inhaled the crisp alpine air and bathed in the glory of the day.

The arctic desert unrolled ahead of us, open and wide, like a flat sand carpet. It was a welcome change from the craggy trails of the previous two days. As we trudged on, the wind blew in furtive gusts from all directions, testing our outer defenses. In between blasts, I got hot and removed layers. During drafts, I got cold and put them back on, so I was constantly donning and doffing outerwear. By the time we floundered deeper into the desert, I was freezing with everything I had. I switched out my sports cap for a black buff to shield my face from the wind and dust.

My stomach started feeling queasy. I didn't know if it stemmed from the high altitude or something I ate or drank. In any event, I had to lumber on despite the discomfort. While I wasn't hungry, perhaps it was my blood sugar. I ate a protein bar and felt somewhat better.

For long stretches, we were alone, with nothing and no one in sight but the massive sandstone cliffs and the vast, barren landscape. We plodded through the angular light of the afternoon toward a rock formation on the distant horizon.

"About another hour," Rutta said.

"It doesn't look that far away," I remarked.

When there is nothing else around for miles, I guess anything appears relatively close.

After some time, we arrived at the outcropping and took shelter from the cutting winds. With my unsettled stomach, I didn't feel like eating the boxed lunch of baked chicken, chips, and juice, but I did anyway, knowing I needed the nourishment. On the flip side, I relished the steaming cup of sweet tea, savoring the warmth it provided to my cold, weary body. I sat back and stared up at the sky, where ravens encircled us, hoping we would feed them some of our rations.

I shifted my gaze to the horizon, where I saw Camp Kibo in the distance, hopeful we would get there soon. Little did we know, it would take us two more hours to arrive. The wind at last subsided, and I got uncomfortably warm again.

The trail veered to the north and evolved into a long, steady incline, appearing almost flat to the casual observer. Yet the gradient belied the difficulty of the slope. In some ways, it was trickier to navigate than the ascents we had encountered before. The propensity was to plod on at a faster pace, particularly as we neared Kibo. But a consistent two- or three-percent gradient over a few miles nearing fifteen thousand feet can be as exhausting as a short, steep ascent at a lower altitude. At least with a sharp rise, one can rest at the top. With this hill, there was no rest, no reprieve. I had to bear down, fighting gale and gravity, with the onslaught of powdery dust lashing my face. The long drag sucked the air out of me and nearly reduced me to a crawl. The only way to conquer it was to power through it—one step at a time. I stopped to drink water and eat fruit, hoping the liquid and fructose would reenergize me.

After what seemed like hours, we arrived at Kibo, the final

staging area and last physical outpost for the summit attempt, in the late afternoon, where my excited friends and I took photos next to the Kibo sign. We had made it to 15,485 feet! When I go back and watch the narrated videos of my journey, I see I was somewhat loopy, having difficulty formulating sentences. I don't think my brain was getting enough oxygen. But I had to remember we climbed higher than any place in the contiguous United States, of which the summit of Mt. Whitney in California is the highest at 14,505 feet. I was even 5,500 feet higher than when I went skydiving a few months before!

I was so grateful to take off my sweaty, dusty clothes, drink some water, and set down my backpack. It had been a long day, but I didn't know we hadn't even tackled the hardest part.

Unlike the days before when we hiked during the day, we had to start our ascent to the summit right before midnight. At night, the glacier is frozen solid, and slippage is less likely. During the day, the sun melts the ice and snow, making the ground slushy and tenable. Firmer earth also makes quicker progress. The plan was to reach the summit before daybreak, enjoy the view for a few minutes as the sun rises, and hurry back down to Kibo Camp before the ground became unstable.

Before dinner, I befriended some climbers from the other groups. One man told me he was with a charitable group providing treatments for the blind, and he was climbing Kilimanjaro since he was already in Africa. That is what I loved about Africa—all the foreigners traveled here either for adventure or humanitarian efforts, and often both. It made me want to get more involved in charitable works.

* * *

WE HAD FOUR HOURS TO sleep before waking up at eleven p.m. to trek to the summit—as if my sleeping schedule wasn't jacked up enough being eight time zones away from home. In only six hours, we would make the swift ascent from 15,485 feet to 19,341 feet. We first convened in the mess hall to eat dinner, but I had no appetite. At high altitude, the body burns on average six thousand calories per day, and it's difficult to replace all that lost energy. Compounded with a loss in appetite, eating and drinking was just another chore, and several of us became afflicted with gastrointestinal issues.

"Hollie, you need to eat," Mary said.

"I don't feel hungry," I told her, even though I knew she was right. I had to force myself.

"You need to eat more," she told me.

"I don't think I can," I said. "My stomach feels so sick."

"Have you taken Diamox?"

"I took some this morning," I said.

"How much?" Mary asked.

"Hmm . . . I took two tablets, 250 milligrams a piece," I said.

"That's too much," she said.

"Really? That is what my doctor prescribed," I told her.

"I think you may have overdosed on Diamox," she said.

I didn't know if that were the case, but it was possible. I had also come down with a cold or some other upper-respiratory ailment, and the congestion did nothing to help my breathing. I had to keep clearing my nose.

Rutta walked over to our table. "We are going to get a reading on you to make sure you have enough oxygen to make the climb."

He went around one by one, and everyone passed the test. He

got to me and said, "Let me have your hand."

After multiple attempts, he could not get a reading on me. Great, I was no longer registering as alive.

"Are you okay to go?" he asked me.

"Yes," I said, still rattling from the frigid air.

There was no way I had come this far and wasn't going to climb.

CHAPTER 31

Stars on Kilimanjaro

Mount Kilimanjaro
June 20, 2017 – Day 3

WE WENT TO BED AROUND seven p.m., the whole group settling into bunk beds in one common area. I tried to write in my journal, but the ink in my pen had frozen, and I could barely make a mark. Even dressed in three layers of clothing, huddled in my sleeping bag, I was painfully cold. In fact, I couldn't remember ever feeling so cold.

The wind whistled from every crack in the ceiling and rattled the windows. With no heat source in our cabin and no vegetation to block the relentless winds of the desert, I might as well have been lying outside, exposed to the elements. *This is primitive. No, it's worse than primitive.* Early humans warmed up by fire. We had no fire. Earth, air, fire, and water. Weren't those the essential elements? I had earth and water in abundance, hardly any air, and no fire. Moreover, sleep at such a high elevation is intermittent and sketchy at best, and I kept dozing off and reawakening.

My mind raced as I lay awake, flipping from one side to the other, hoping a particular position would warm me up. On top of that, the frequent hydration kept me going to the outhouse. Each time, I had to grab my flashlight, and creep one hundred feet down a jagged, rocky slope, each step making me wince with pain and gasp for air. The furious winds whipped at me, nearly knocking me over.

When was it ever this hard to go to the damn bathroom? My hands were freezing, so I had to wear my thick Gore-Tex gloves. When I got to the outhouse, I took off the bulky gloves and inadvertently dropped one of them into the pit. *Shit!* The premium gloves my mother had bought me! The ones that were supposed to keep my hands warm as I climbed to the summit! *Well, crap! That's gone.*

When I returned outside, I breathed in the coppery smell of desert dust and looked up at the never-ending sea of stars, flashing and flickering like ice crystals. A delicate crescent moon cradled the dim, ghostly outline of its complete self. It was so quiet I could hear the falling of a quill, the squeak of a door, and the sound of the night itself breathing through the mild zephyrs. Maybe it was worth going out in the numbing cold of the desert to see this. I wasn't sleeping, anyway. A few minutes later, I traipsed back to the cabin and curled up in my sleeping bag, where I drifted off into a light, unproductive sleep.

Two hours later, our guides awoke us, exclaiming, "It's time to go!" I felt like I had not slept at all. I was bone-weary and exhausted from climbing at an ever-increasing altitude and trying to keep myself warm. And my head was still congested with cold-like symptoms.

We began our final surge to the peak at midnight with headlamps affixed to our heads. I was wrapped in three layers of clothing, a face mask, and my one glove. Almost immediately, I struggled to breathe as I plodded up the steep grade. I had to stop every few steps to gasp for air. My group's excited chatter gave way to silence as we trudged onward, the only sound the shuffling of our feet.

Unlike the previous days, the trails never leveled off. The slope of the mountain up to this point was gentle compared to what lay before us. No switchbacks relieved us by making the climb gradual. It was steep and unrelenting. I tried to use a technique I often use in running, where I tell myself to make it to the next tree or signpost. However, there was nothing to latch on to in the perpetual darkness. I thought, *Hollie, you've trekked mountains dozens of times. It can't be that hard.*

I fixed my gaze on a row of seven stars ahead, hoping their pull on me was somehow magnetic. Moments later, though, I realized those "stars" were the headlamps of climbers before me. I tried to make it to the crest of each hill, yet as soon as I reached the "top," it continued. It was like ancient voyagers trying to find the precipitous edge of a seemingly flat Earth. I was chasing the horizon, only to find it never ended.

I started feeling lethargic and lightheaded. About every minute, I paused to catch my breath, swallowing the oxygen-deficient air. I lagged farther behind my group, and they had to wait for me. Rutta asked me to move to the front of the pack, so I would not fall behind. Even then, I kept stopping to catch my breath, and I felt like I was holding the group back.

Zebadiah, a kindhearted guide who was old enough to be my father, took my backpack for me, and Rutta made me drink some Coke. A harsh, chilly wind, reminiscent of the gusts in Oklahoma, cut through all my layers. I trudged on, but was feeling worse.

Rutta saw I was struggling and asked, "Would you like to turn back?"

"No," I told him. "I can do it."

After coming this far, I wasn't going to backtrack now.

He said Zeb could escort me at my own pace, which seemed like the ideal solution. While the slower pace was better, I was becoming faint, and I was wobbling. My legs nearly gave out from under me, but fortunately, Zeb caught me. If it weren't for Zeb and my trekking poles, I would have tumbled several times over the jagged trail.

The mountain clenched me and wouldn't let me go. One endless footstep after another. *One step, two steps, three steps, four steps. Stop. Breathe. Repeat.* Black stars clouded my vision, and I began to feel dizzy. In my delirium, I saw an animal that looked like an armadillo with black and white stripes. *A zebra armadillo? Is there such a thing?* But it vanished as quickly as it appeared. A moment later, we came across another group of hikers, and I saw a monkey on a man's back. When I got closer, I realized it was a backpack. I knew almost no mammals besides humans inhabited this altitude. The lack of oxygen and vegetation made the area unsustainable. I chuckled and thought, *This must be what it's like to trip out on LSD!*

Nausea, insomnia, vertigo, fatigue, loss of appetite—the worst symptoms of altitude sickness. I stood hunched over, gulping for air and feeling nauseated from the exertion and the altitude. With each step I took, the mountain pushed back with greater force. *Am I in control of my body anymore?*

The human mind is a wellspring of fortitude. It is not only capable of second winds, but also third and fourth winds, and even more when necessary. The difference between endurance athletes and casual athletes is the ability to tap into mental reserves again and again and force the body to listen. It is a brutal test of willpower. I had found my replenishments before, and I could do it now. Running marathons had trained me to uncover my absolute physical limits.

I thought I had reached that edge before—until now.

As I continued to ascend, I felt the weight of the mountain on my chest, and my mind seemed to separate from my depleted body. With each step, I felt like I could not go on. The freezing wind cut right through my glove, and my red hands stung from the unflagging pain. I kept flexing my fingers to regain some circulation. I looked over at Zeb and his kind, weather-beaten face, who had taken this journey dozens of times. He took my hands in his and rubbed them, trying to warm them up. I tried to sip water from my hydration pack, only to discover the water in the dispensing tube had frozen. I had water, but no way to access it. *Great.*

After three hours of stopping and starting, we took refuge in Hans Meyer cave, the halfway point, at seventeen thousand feet. Sheltered temporarily in the cave, Zeb gave me some hot tea, the sweet elixir warming my hands as well as my insides.

I knew this was a pivotal moment.

Do I keep pushing myself?

I thought about my freezing hands, throbbing with pain, my frozen water pack, and the suffocating air. I thought about my legs giving out from extreme exhaustion, my dizzy spells, and the hallucinations. *If I turn around, am I giving up?* I thought of how hard and long I had trained. For months, for years, perhaps my entire life, I had prepared for this moment. But Kilimanjaro was not kidding around. If I finished, it would easily be the most rigorous feat I had ever undertaken.

Wait, it already was. No marathon I had run even compared.

Although reaching the summit was a dream of mine, none of my training had primed me for this. I gazed at the night sky, searching the Universe for an answer. I thought of my loved ones who had already parted the earth—my father and my two stepfathers—to channel their wisdom.

The Universe whispered to me, *Hollie, you know the answer.*

At that point, I knew what I needed to do.

I turned to Zeb and said, "Let's go back." I knew I could not go another three hours, and the air was only getting thinner. I could keep forcing myself and possibly risk endangering my life. It was one thing to feel exhausted; it was another matter not to be able to breathe. My lungs felt like they were about to burst.

As Zeb and I started our descent, I beheld a yellow crescent moon hanging from the dome of the star-crowded sky. I looked up into the heavens and gazed upon an ocean of infinite depth, millions of dazzling suns rollicking in their celestial dance. The universe stretched out before me, unbounded and whole. During this interlude, I felt no suffering or discomfort, just complete and profound peace.

The night sky transformed from navy to fluorescent blue, the unrisen sun illuminating the volcanic peaks. Even though I hadn't slept in over twenty-four hours and was dehydrated, nauseous, and exhausted, I felt enraptured. This is what I came for—not only to get to the summit but to behold this heavenly spectacle.

Oxygen returned to my lungs as I gulped the precious, life-giving air. Little by little, I felt my life force returning to me. When we arrived back at Kibo Camp two hours later, Zeb gave me an enormous hug. Even though I did not make it to the peak, I celebrated completing the greatest physical challenge of my life! When I collapsed in bed, night had progressed well into the morning. Grateful to breathe again, drowsiness overtook me, and I fell into a deep, dreamless sleep, losing my sense of place and time.

CHAPTER 32

Descent

Mount Kilimanjaro
June 21, 2017 – Day 4

I AWOKE A COUPLE OF hours later, stiff and cold, to the faint orange glow of morning irradiating through the window. Days were no longer defined by sunrise and sunset, nor by hours on the clock, but by the ceaseless flow of time itself. I had watched the sun, moon, and stars move in a continuous arc across the sky, leaving behind a blurry reflection of the millions of details I had assimilated. I had long lost track of the date and the day of the week, or how much time had passed. If anything, the days overlapped, one spilling into the next, so that I didn't know when one day ended and another began. To my body, the last few celestial cycles had been one long, unceasing duration.

I crawled out of my sleeping bag, covered my head, and stepped outside. Both exhaustion and excitement consumed me as I absorbed the wonder of my surroundings. My home, ten thousand miles away, seemed as distant as the stars descending on the skyline.

I looked to the summit with newfound respect. Kilimanjaro is as noble and enticing as she is rugged and unforgiving. Despite what we'd like to think, we are not masters of the mountain.

I paced outside and scanned the northern slopes of leaden volcanic rock carved by wind and glaciers, waiting for my friends to emerge. By the time they returned, it had taken them eight hours to reach the summit before returning to Kibo Camp. Charlie, the man who had run over one hundred marathons, said it was physically the most challenging thing he had ever done. I am confident I wouldn't have had six hours left in me to make it to the summit and felt reaffirmed I had made the right decision. After a simple breakfast, we packed our belongings to begin our descent.

* * *

WHAT HAD TAKEN US FOUR days to surmount took only two days to trek down. The slopes that had been so grueling only a day before came more easily as we inhaled more oxygen. Even so, they were challenging in a different way. Descending the rutted, rocky trails put excruciating stress on my knees, even with my trekking poles to absorb some of the shock. Each step shot a spasm of agony up my leg. I started singing to distract myself, while muttering a torrent of expletives.

"Are you okay?" asked Rutta. "You're not keeping up with the rest of the group."

"What happened to '*pole, pole*'?" I asked him. "I am old, and my knees hurt."

Behind me, loud shuffling caught my attention, and I turned around. Two porters whisked past us with climbers in gurneys. As I peered more closely, I saw it was Chris and Saint!

"Are they going to be all right?" I asked Rutta.

"Yes, they will be okay," he said. "They went farther than the rest of the group and made it to Uhuru Peak, but they are exhausted."

Holy crap! They were the youngest, fittest people in our group. I thanked the Universe again that I made the right choice. That could have been me on that gurney had I continued to push toward the summit.

By late afternoon, we made our way back to Horombo, the encampment on the clouds, where we collapsed in our cabins and drifted into a full night's sleep.

June 22, 2017 – Day 5

AS WE REENTERED THE MOORLAND, I felt something I had not felt in days—hunger! The altitude *had* been affecting my appetite. When Jimmy pulled out a Snickers bar, it looked like the most mouthwatering food I had ever seen.

"Do you have another one of those?" I asked him, my eyes popping out.

He reached into his bag and handed me one. I devoured it like a voracious dog. It was the most delicious thing I had tasted in days, and Snickers is not even my favorite candy bar.

After eight hours, we arrived back at Mandara Hut, where we slumbered our last night on Kilimanjaro.

CHAPTER 33

The Return

Mount Kilimanjaro
June 23, 2017 – Day 6

OUTSIDE MANDARA, A FINE MIST rose in the stream of early-morning sunlight, dissipating into the tropical breeze. As we made our way back through the stillness of the rainforest, our footsteps crunched on the wet carpet of leaves and twigs. A fine drizzle shrouded the leaves and branches, the tops of the trees disappearing into the ethereal mist. In some places, the dense overhanging canopy of trees made it seem like twilight.

When we were about an hour away from the entrance to the trailhead, some porters brought us boxes of food with a meat-filled pastry, similar to an empanada. The decadent, crunchy exterior and tender, succulently-spiced chicken were roasted to perfection. I sat on the trunk of a fallen tree and enjoyed the meal with my newfound appetite.

As we edged on, a glowing light loomed in the distance, beckoning us closer. It was the Marangu exit, the end of our journey! As we emerged from the forest and crossed the threshold back into civilization, throngs of people cheered, embracing us and taking our photos. Celebrating at the picnic table with a feast of fried chicken, potatoes, fruit salad, and wine, my friends and I beamed and raised our glasses to each other. We had made it!

As we traveled back, we passed through the same villages and scenes we had during the beginning of our journey, but everything looked and felt different. I *was* different.

At our hotel in Moshi, I looked in the mirror and barely recognized myself. My lips were cracked. My red skin was crusted over, weather-beaten, and covered with grime and mosquito bites. When I touched my face, it felt scratchy and leathery, sandblasted by the furious gusts of dry wind and numbing cold. Part of me thought I looked ghastly, but another part of me took pride in my haggard appearance. For the past seven days, I had lived an experience far more remarkable than I could have imagined.

CHAPTER 34
Mount Kilimanjaro Marathon

Moshi, Tanzania
June 25, 2017

THERE WAS NO QUESTION: I was going to run the full marathon, even though I had not run more than twelve miles continuously in the last year. I could blame it on the corrupt influence of my new running friends—in particular, Charlie—or maybe my head was not functioning properly after climbing Kilimanjaro. Marathoners often aren't right in the head, anyway. If Charlie, the man the locals affectionately called *Babu*—grandpa in Swahili—could run it after all we had done, so could I.

I floundered in my bed, both nervous and excited, the blaring music from a wedding reception right outside my window keeping me awake. On another night, I might have crashed the party, like I did one night in New York's Central Park a few years ago. But if the revelers caroused all night, I might not get any rest and be left to nothing but the anxious thoughts I was already having. *What if I have to drop out? What if my knees give out during the marathon?* They had taken such a beating on the mountain, and I still winced when I walked. I couldn't worry about that, though. I had run through injuries before, and I could do it again.

To my relief, it started pouring around midnight, putting an immediate damper on the party. The windows of my room rattled, as the raindrops lashed against the panes. While I was grateful that the celebration wrapped up, I was also concerned it would rain during the marathon.

Early in the morning, the drumming of the rain on the flat roof woke me. It had been showering all night. Dressing in my running singlet and shorts of blue, yellow, and green, the same colors as the Tanzanian flag, I peered out at Kilimanjaro, grateful for the strength she had shown me. I needed it for my race today. After eating a light breakfast and downing four ibuprofen, I met my friends outside to catch the bus to the starting line. By good fortune, the rain had ceased. The coach that was supposed to transport us, however, broke down, and we arrived at the starting line in front of the Moshi Club fifteen minutes late. In other places, the marathon would have started without us, but this was Tanzania, where no one hurried.

When we exited the bus, electricity filled the air. Several local Tanzanians and visitors from countries all over the world chattered about the race. I did a Facebook Live video for my friends and family back in the US, interviewing some of the runners. I introduced Mary to my Facebook audience.

"We're going to kick butt today!" she told everyone.

Next, I introduced Charlie, who was running in place with a Tanzanian runner he had befriended.

"I am pacing him for the first twelve feet!" Charlie exclaimed.

"I hope you can keep up with him," I said to the Tanzanian, laughing.

Finally, I introduced Christy and Paul, a young couple from Minnesota, whom I had just met the night before at dinner. They had not yet climbed Kilimanjaro, opting to run the marathon first.

"It's cooler here than in Minnesota," they said.

Cooler in the tropics? Maybe we would end up with optimal running weather.

The dirt road we had surveyed for the course the day before had morphed into a muddy morass. In the twenty-seven years the marathon had operated, it was one of the few times it had rained. In a way, it helped us because it ended the raucous wedding party, but the muck was going to be a challenge. The one and only time I had run a race in the mud was my first cross country race when I was fourteen years old. My feet slipped out of my shoes when I tried to disentangle them from the quagmire. I hoped my feet wouldn't get stuck on this course. By good luck, the course was part mud and part pavement, consisting of four 10-kilometer loops.

I anxiously lined up on the starting line, about to run my eighth marathon. I stared down at the rippled muscles in my legs, the culmination of the thousands of miles I had run, the legs that had nearly carried me to the roof of Africa, and I felt a surge of power.

The race director, yelled, "Go!"

We sprinted out, flinging mud behind us with each stride. *Who cares if it was a little grimy?* It wasn't like I hadn't been filthy for the past week.

After about a mile, we made it to the pavement and entered the city streets. Local policemen controlled the traffic, so we could pass by. The drivers probably wondered who the crazy people were out running. A light drizzle descended upon us, which helped to keep us cool.

Three miles into the first loop, I reached another unpaved part of the road that wound through a wooded section of town, replete with shacks, dogs, and barefoot children. I waved at the children as I passed and paused at the first water stop, run by the local seminarians. By the end of the first 10K loop, my knees were holding up, and I still felt great!

By the time I passed the Moshi Club again at the start of the second loop, my shoes were caked in mud anew. With the drizzle, the road had become exceptionally sticky, and I tried to run on the outer edges, where the grass could give me some traction. I had to stop and scrape my shoes off when I reached the pavement again.

When I arrived at the crowded intersection again, the local police had disappeared, leaving us to fend for ourselves out in the traffic. Part of the loop required a turnaround, so I was able to see my friends running in the opposite direction up a mile-long hill, where we could cheer each other on. While the way down felt great, running up was brutal.

At the end of the second loop, I took some salt tablets to replenish my electrolytes. With the clouds moving out, it heated up quickly. Since the streets in Moshi are not lined with grass, dust saturates the air. Passing cars, flinging dirt from the street and blowing exhaust fumes in my face, sent me into coughing spasms, momentarily choking me.

By the end of the third loop (about mile 20), I still felt outstanding, except for the salt from my sweat that burned my eyes. On all the previous marathons I had run, I usually started wearing down at mile 17, and by mile 20 felt like I was going to drop. I had just one more loop. I power walked the long hill to conserve my energy, as the heat and humidity became more oppressive.

At long last, I crossed the finish line, my legs plastered with mud. Nelson, one of the local runners, lifted me up in celebration.

"How do you feel, Ms. Hollie?" he asked me in his Tanzanian accent.

"I feel fuckin' amazing!" I exclaimed.

That is what I love most about running. My entire life, it has reminded me in my toughest moments, I am strong.

Afterward, I celebrated at the Moshi Club alongside Saint, Chris, Mark, and Shawn with a glass bottle of Coke, fried chicken, and fries. Mary, Charlie, Paul, and Christy finished shortly after. At the awards ceremony later, I found out I had finished number one female overall for the marathon—a first for me!

But that's not what made the event so wonderful. It was the friendships I had built. During experiences like this, boundaries collapse, and masks come down. Divergent opinions, beliefs, worldviews, and lifestyles don't matter. We are all humans who survived an extraordinary undertaking together, and we forge bonds different from everyday existence. It was going to be hard to say goodbye to everyone.

CHAPTER 35
Unbounded

Prison Island, Zanzibar, Tanzania
July 4, 2017

As we approached Prison Island, the white caps on the water settled to ripples, and the light, saline breeze tousled my hair. Glassy, aquamarine waters enveloped expanses of white sand beaches and thick tracts of flourishing forest. Boats swayed along the pier, waves lapping against their sides, and a coral reef created mottled shadows in the pristine, turquoise water.

After we disembarked, Newman led me down a cobbled path to the 121-year-old prison ruins. Rather than surveying a dingy closed-in structure, I found myself in an open courtyard with an outdoor cocktail lounge. I had difficulty discerning the gold-tinged stone walls through the overgrowth of red and pink bougainvillea that cascaded down the walls. Only upon closer inspection could I discern the barred windows that yielded a stunning view of the steep cliffs, shallow coves, patches of beach, and the endless blue ocean. The cool breeze from the water lifted my hair from my neck and soothed my frazzled nerves. Placing my hand on the warm, rough-hewn wall, I gazed out at sea.

"This doesn't look like a prison. Where were the prisoners held?" I asked Newman, puzzled.

He laughed. "It never actually held prisoners. It was supposed to at first, but then it was used as a quarantine station for yellow fever. Later it was converted into a resort."

Maybe I would have been less anxious had I known that.

Newman and I padded away from the old prison courtyard and entered an indoor lounge, tucked away in one of the nearby alcoves. The lounge was light, airy, and swathed in sunlight. Brown padded seats and pillows lined the walls. Lazy motes of dust filtered through the rays, reflecting off the bright yellow textured walls. I lay on the sofa, extending my arms along the back. A breeze navigated its way through the blue shuttered windows and riffed through the pages of an open book on the table. The walls depicted two lovely murals of a woman in a black burqa and a man in a black kufi. Inhaling the salty sea air, I allowed myself to relish the moment.

* * *

THE OTHER SIDE OF THE islet hosted a spectacular utopia of color and wildlife. To my delight, the towering canopies of trees provide a sanctuary for peacocks, butterflies, and the giant Aldabra tortoises, classified as a vulnerable species. The tortoises huddled together, sharing a meal of leafy greens.

"Would you like to feed a tortoise?" Newman asked. "This one is 192 years old."

"Absolutely!" I said.

I crouched down and held some greens about an inch from the tortoise's beak.

"Here you go, big guy," I said in my sweet baby-talk voice.

He inched over and started crunching on the stems. To feed a rare, giant tortoise out in the wild that is almost two centuries old—what a thrill!

* * *

AFTER DEPARTING THE REFUGE, I told Newman, "I want to dip my feet in the water!"

When we approached the shore, I plunged my feet into the sand and felt the waves of the Indian Ocean splash my shins. I stood in the water, myriad shades of green, blue, sapphire, emerald, and teal nudging my legs. Legions of fish brushed against my toes and tickled my calves, a thousand darting, glistening flashes of color against the white sand. I had nearly touched the roof of Africa, and now here I was treading the continent's floor out in the open sea. My feet had taken me on an incredible journey from base to peak to basin.

When I was thirteen years old, the power of my body was taken from me. As I worked to reclaim it, I could feel the energy and strength of each of its movements. My legs represent my individual path, my uniqueness, my strength, and my independent spirit. My arms embody my connection to others and my belonging to the human race. When I am running, especially during adventure marathons, I am both overwhelmed and awed by the vastness of the distance before me, which I must traverse using only the power of my body. Running to distant horizons in Tanzania, on the Inca Trail, the Great Wall of China, and the Himalayas, I can see for miles all around me and feel a wondrous connection to the infinity of the universe. I feel the entire cosmos enveloping me in its radiant splendor.

The Universe had given me all I ever needed and wanted—and more. If someone had told me when I was a young girl in Pawhuska that I would one day ride camelback across the Sahara, go on safari through the Serengeti, trek the Inca Trail, hike the Himalayas, run the Great Wall of China, and climb Mount Kilimanjaro, I don't know that I would have believed it.

I laughed, thinking I was getting kidnapped an hour before. I had lived in my own self-imposed prison for years, girdled in shame and self-loathing. Just as I had discovered on Prison Island, what I had thought was a prison wasn't a prison at all.

In spring of 1989, when I was asked to give the class graduation speech, I was braving one of the bleakest moments of my life. It was mere months after the assault, when I didn't know who I was anymore. I couldn't imagine what my future might look like. I couldn't even see myself beyond the month, much less years into the future.

Now, for the first time, the shackles around me disappeared. A heavy burden lifted from me, and in that placid state, a soothing thought entered my mind. I never had anything to atone for. I didn't have to prove anything to anyone, not even myself. The revelation filled me with so much joy that I found myself leaning back with arms outstretched, welcoming the sun's embrace. As if awakening from a long sleep, my soul was once again free and unbounded. I had emerged from unfathomable depths, and I could see for miles and miles.

EPILOGUE

July 2022

ALTHOUGH THE CLIMB UP MOUNT Kilimanjaro didn't turn out how I thought it would, I learned so much about myself. Had I done the climb a few months before, I would have felt like I had something to prove to myself and to other people. I would have been disappointed by not making the summit. Instead, I am proud of pushing myself to the edge without going over it. My self-worth didn't hinge on reaching the peak.

Since my experience on Kilimanjaro, I have learned more about climbing the seven summits. According to Rutta, I was certainly fit enough to summit Kilimanjaro, but I had not sufficiently acclimatized to the high altitude. Ascending four thousand feet in a few hours to 19,341 feet is ambitious by any standards. He said I would have fared better had I taken one of the longer routes.

Even with Mount Everest, the world's tallest peak, climbers don't go for the summit in one shot. They constantly ascend and descend to acclimatize, each time going progressively higher. The best way to acclimatize is not to climb too far, too fast to allow the body to adjust to the decreased oxygen levels. Since climbers are already working at maximum capacity, the risk increases for pulmonary or cerebral edema, which can be fatal.

* * *

WHILE CLIMBING KILIMANJARO FULFILLED A dream, I still had work to do. I told my mother, who I talked to almost every day, that I was writing a memoir, part of which included my story of the assault. Anytime I brought it up, she was not enthused and changed the subject. After all, I was violating an implicit family code: Don't talk about these things publicly. Notwithstanding, I made it clear to her that I was not asking for her approval. It was something I felt called to do. Shame thrives in secrecy, and the only way to mitigate it is to shine a big-ass light on it. If even one person can benefit from my story, it is worth it to me. As much as I yearned for my mother's support, it appeared I would walk this road without her.

I discerned a change in my mother, however, during Brett Kavanaugh's confirmation hearing for the US Supreme Court in 2018. One day, she came over to my house and commented she felt sorry for Judge Kavanaugh. She said she would feel awful if anyone accused her sons of assault.

"What about your daughters who have been assaulted?" I asked.

The story of Dr. Ford, Kavanaugh's accuser, was eerily close to mine, and the way people eviscerated and discredited her was gut-wrenching for me.

"Watching this hearing and the way people are treating her has been really hard for me," I said.

"I'm so sorry, honey," she said and hugged me.

For once, Mom didn't dismiss or minimize my pain. She sat on the couch with me and held me.

"I should have been there to protect you," she said.

"Mom, it's not your fault. I've never blamed you. You couldn't be everywhere with us. You did the best you could."

* * *

IN 2019, I WROTE A chapter for a women's anthology called *Ready to Fly,* where I began to share my story. Publishing the chapter was one of the most frightening things I have ever done. Even though my mother was beginning to understand, I still felt like I was opposing her. In my work with Lauren, my current therapist, and Jill, my coach, I got to a point I didn't need my mother's validation of what happened. I no longer needed my family to understand me. I understood myself, and that's what matters. Ironically, once I reached that point, my mother called me and said, "I love you, and I am so proud of you, and I want you to know I support you." That was all she ever had to say to me. I didn't need her permission anymore, but getting her blessing meant the world to me. I had long given up I would ever hear those words, and it brought me to tears.

When I reflect on my mother's response to my abuse, I remind myself it clashed with everything she knew, everything she had been taught. Seventy-six years of conditioning. If I thought it was hard for me to unlearn over forty years of misinformation and cultural conditioning, I imagine it was that much harder for my mother, who had to unlearn over seventy years of it.

The schools didn't have the right information, either. In the religious schools I attended, there was a singular focus on sexual morality and not committing sin, rather than teaching kids to respect other people's boundaries. I experienced firsthand the adverse effect that religious education can have when it is not balanced. I have also spoken with my friends to get their impressions on our education, and they have expressed that sexuality was discussed mainly in the context of sin, and they still contend with shame like I do, even without experiencing assault. I don't believe that was the intention of our school, but it was the outcome. Comprehensive sex education, including what constitutes consent, would have been much more helpful. However, it is still not mandated in public or religious institutions in 2022, much less was it in 1988. With the #MeToo movement, it has gained more traction, but not to the level that's required.

Education has been instrumental in my healing. In becoming more knowledgeable, I am not only healing myself, but the generations of women who came before me. I want the cultural programming to end with me so that I can pass on new information to my nieces and nephew. I want to help inspire dialogue on what constitutes aggression and abuse, so that it's not so deeply woven into our culture. In retrospect, if I had been provided greater knowledge and awareness, better tools and guides, my suffering could have been dramatically diminished. I hope that women who have been through similar experiences will read my story, find their own power and agency, and most importantly, know they don't have to suffer in silence.

By healing myself and telling my story, I also hope to help current and future generations. I want girls and women to know that their worth is not tied up in any violence they may experience or in their sexuality.

* * *

ON SEPTEMBER 9, 2019, JILL AND I had a book signing at Full Circle Bookstore in Oklahoma City to promote *Ready to Fly*. I had never been more nervous in my life. I was about to disclose what had happened to me in front of my extended family, my classmates from high school, and my mother. It was like coming out of the closet. *What are they going to think of me?* It may or may not have been consistent with how they had always known me. Then I reminded myself why I was doing it.

When I was finished speaking, several members of the audience came up to me and thanked me for telling my story and had me sign the book. My mother approached me, beaming with pride, and said, "I am so *proud* of you." Even though I had moved from a place I didn't need to hear that, it was the loveliest thing she ever said to me. In that moment, the space between us closed, and a tenderness and understanding unfurled where there had been so much pain and misunderstanding.

Little did I know how precious that moment would become. Fewer than three months later, on December 5, 2019, my mother passed away unexpectedly from a heart attack. The moment I had feared my whole life had come. She disappeared from my life with no warning, just like my father and John had. After the initial shock and devastation of her passing, I saw her support as one of the greatest gifts she could have given me. So many friends told me afterward that my mother was the proudest person in that room. After three years of struggling to help her understand, it seemed almost unreal. At long last, she had come around and fully supported me.

Almost a year after my mother passed, I was going through her items and found the letter she had written me when I was fourteen years old, mere months after the assault. It said:

Dear Hollie,

This letter is to tell you how much I love you. When you were born, I thought you were the most beautiful baby girl, and you were. You've grown up now, and you're still beautiful and a wonderful person. I couldn't ask for a better daughter. I'm so proud of the kind of person you are. I hope you'll always come to me if you ever need anything or ever have a problem you need help with. I love you just because you're you!

Mom

I broke down sobbing. She loved me when I felt the worst about myself and thought I had failed her. The story I had told myself was all wrong. She was proud of me—then and always. Our love for each other was as pure and infinite as it was the day I was born.

Nearly my entire life, I believed things that weren't true: The assaults were my fault. I must have deserved them. I must have been a bad person. Something was wrong with me. I was unlovable. I disappointed my mother. I had lost part of myself.

None of it is true.

* * *

ULTIMATELY, MY TRAUMAS HAVE WHATEVER meaning and purpose I ascribe to them. I get to decide what to do with what happened. I could choose to tell myself the story that I am broken and damaged or that I am whole and loved. It doesn't mean the damage never occurred; I just won't let it define me. I no longer blame the thirteen-year-old girl for the boys who assaulted her, and I don't blame the adults in my life. They couldn't teach me what they didn't know.

I still occasionally experience episodes of depression and PTSD. With the healing I've done and with the proper medications, the occurrences aren't as intense. It's a condition I have that recurs periodically, but now I have tools and the support system to handle it, rather than suffering through it. November is no longer a dreaded time of year for me. I know the episodes will pass, and they won't kill me.

With each loss I have experienced, I have, in turn, gained so much. Had events transpired differently, I wouldn't know many of the wonderful people I do now. I have learned to have compassion for my younger self, who was doing her best. And just because I was struggling didn't mean I was failing. I can endure my darkest moments and still survive. Now when I seek to improve myself, it does not come from a place of shame, self-loathing, or perceived penance. It comes from a place of self-love and seeking to be the best Hollie I can be.

While my life didn't unfold exactly like I thought it would, I get to do all the things I dreamed of as a child: going on adventures, visiting exotic locations, experiencing different cultures, and meeting people from all over the world! Being a single woman with no children has also allowed me to pursue a fulfilling career and engage in humanitarian causes. I did not let the assault ruin me; if anything, it deepened my sense of empathy for others. I can now see what my life will be like now that I'm no longer chained to the past.

In the end, I am not my achievements nor my apparent failures. I am not my depression and PTSD. I am not the assault or anything else that has happened to me. I am and always have been HoHo.

Thank you for taking the time to read my story! If you enjoyed *I Can See for Miles,* please leave a review through the provided link or QR code below. As an independent author, I rely heavily on word-of-mouth recommendations and support from readers like you. Thank you for being a part of my journey!

Sincerely,

Hollie

https://bitly.ws/Zp3v

ACKNOWLEDGMENTS

I labored away at this book for five years and often wondered if I would ever finish. Thanks to those of you who encouraged me to keep going and reminded me why I am telling my story.

I am grateful to my editor Kristen Hamilton, who helped me with big picture and scene development. Without her, my story would have digressed from the main narrative. I am indebted to my beta readers, who read the final working draft and offered valuable feedback to improve the story: Elizabeth Fortune, Dinky Hammam, Dan Yates, Erica Erickson, Kara Uhlenbrock, Lisa Kingsley, and Staci Craig. It is infinitely better because of them. I am also thankful to Victoria Wolfe for the stunning cover design and to Crystal MM Burton for the creative interior design.

So many people have affirmed and supported me on my journey, not just in writing the book, but in my life. I couldn't include everyone who has played an important role in my story, so I include them here:

My mother Sandra Stuart Price, who always reminded me I have a special place in the world and never let me forget it

My fathers DJ Stuart, John Price, and Bob Craig for guiding me and picking up where the previous one left off

My grandmother Jane Thompson, who continues to surround me with her white light

My sister Kelley Fuechsel, for her unflagging support of me telling my story and her permission to relate any details of her life pertaining to mine

My aunts Nancy Hardeman and Diane Burgess

David Morton

Mary Jane Rapp Scharnberg

Sister Sheila Carroll

Ken Doake

Patricia Roussell

Jill Keuth

Dee Mathis

Lissette Norris

Crystal Blue

Carol Koss

Laurie Kenney

Lauren Rieken-Hobbs

Jennifer Sweeton

Courtney Nixon

Laura Teske

Heather Reck

Miganoush Grigorian

Amanda Levine

Claudia Crow

Leslie Buck

Sarah Iglesias

Mike McVey

Jody Entwistle

And, of course, I give heartfelt thanks to my extended family, my running family, and my Toastmasters family. Your steadfast encouragement has made all the difference.

ABOUT THE AUTHOR

Hollie Stuart is a dual-certified human resources professional and #1 bestselling / award-winning author and keynote speaker. She most recently published her moving memoir *I Can See for Miles*, which has won eight awards, including the 2023 International Book Award, the 2023 Indie Excellence Award, the 2023 Next Generation Indie Book Award, and the 2023 BookFest® Award.

In her memoir and during speaking engagements, Hollie shows people how they can overcome trauma, reclaim their power, and reshape their narrative and identity.

Both professionally and personally, Hollie devotes herself to humanitarian and social causes, advocating for women's empowerment, as well as awareness and prevention of various types of discrimination, harassment, and sexual assault.

An avid world traveler, adventurer, marathoner, and outdoors enthusiast, Hollie is fulfilling her goal of running a marathon on all seven continents, most recently completing the 2022 Queenstown Marathon in New Zealand. In 2019, she ran the Great Wall Marathon in China and the Thunder Dragon Marathon in Bhutan only eight days apart. She regales her journey to Tanzania in *I Can See for Miles*, where she completed the 2017 Mount Kilimanjaro Marathon and scaled Mount Kilimanjaro, the tallest freestanding mountain in the world.

In her free time, Hollie looks for ways to embrace the whole spectrum of human experiences and befriend people all over the globe. She has several nieces and nephews, whom she adores, and aspires to be the world's "coolest" aunt.

Hollie holds a Master of Liberal Studies from the University of Oklahoma and resides in the Oklahoma City area.

You can visit Hollie's website at holliestuart.com.

Made in the USA
Coppell, TX
15 February 2024

29064838R00152